Favorable
Executions

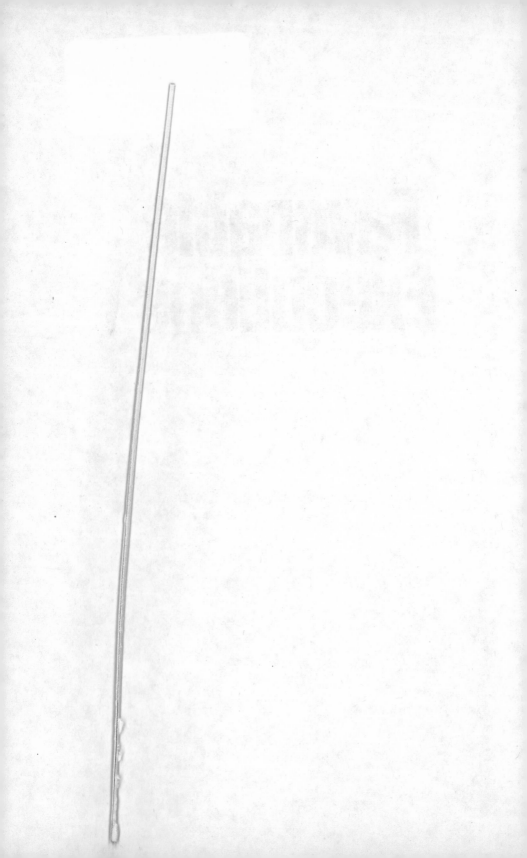

Favorable Executions

THE WALL STREET SPECIALIST AND THE AUCTION MARKET

Michael G. Zahorchak

 VAN NOSTRAND REINHOLD COMPANY
New York   Cincinnati   Toronto   London   Melbourne

3 4 8 8 9 2

HG
4572
.Z34
1974

Van Nostrand Reinhold Company Regional Offices:
New York Cincinnati Chicago Millbrae Dallas

Van Nostrand Reinhold Company International Offices:
London Toronto Melbourne

Copyright © 1974 by Litton Educational Publishing, Inc.

Library of Congress Catalog Card Number: 73-13878
ISBN: 0-442-29571-5

Manufactured in the United States of America

Published by Van Nostrand Reinhold Company
450 West 33rd Street, New York, N.Y. 10001

Published simultaneously in Canada by Van Nostrand Reinhold Ltd.

15 14 13 12 11 10 9 8 7 6 5 4 3 2 1

Library of Congress Cataloging in Publication Data

Zahorchak, Michael G
  Favorable Executions

    1. Stock-exchange—United States. 2. Stocks—
Prices. 3. Brokers. I. Title.
HG4572.Z34   332.6'42'0973   73-13878
ISBN 0-442-29571-5

To
The Men
More to be Admired
Than Admonished

Introduction

For the first time you can look over the specialist's shoulder and see him in action making a market in his stocks. See why stock prices move the way they do. See how a specialist thinks, acts and reacts in response to market pressures. See exactly what makes stocks move up and down. See what a specialist can and cannot do to influence the market price of a stock.

Favorable Executions is a definitive work on stock exchange specialists and the stock market auction process. It takes the reader back to the first known stock exchange in Europe of the 1600s through the present, and the changes being contemplated for the future. It tells of the people involved in making auction markets work, from the promoter who first issues stock in his new venture to the investor or speculator who ultimately trades the stock.

Favorable Executions will prove invaluable in correcting the faulty thinking that leads to so many investment losses. Here a typical specialist explains his philosophy toward the market. See why this one man who is not permitted to back away from markets that usually defeat lesser men, nearly always manages, like a cat, to land on his feet. What does a specialist look for to tell him that a stock is strong and heading higher? What does he look for to tell him there's trouble ahead? Read an expert's advice on how to minimize risks in any kind of market.

Preface

What determines the price you pay when you decide to buy some stock? What sets the price when you sell?

This is a question that for years has both fascinated and disturbed millions of investors. But like the feminine mystique, it has remained an elusive quantity. Most of those who have attempted to answer this question in the past have done no more than scratch the surface. And in scratching the surface, they have seldom come to grips with the soul of the matter.

What determines the price you pay? Why supply and demand, of course! But what is supply? What is demand? And if they are so all fired important why can some investors who really demand stock buy all they want right at the bottom, then sell near the top? Shouldn't their buying raise prices? Then why doesn't it?

The truth of the matter is that we don't know the mystery of the market. Nevertheless we will attempt to understand it by defining the elements which interact to result in the price you pay when you effect a transaction. We will do this by taking you down to the Floor of the American Stock Exchange and letting you look over the shoulders of a stock exchange specialist as he goes about his business. There you will see how the most professional of all market professionals thinks, acts and reacts to the pressures of investors like yourself and how what you do sets the price level of a stock.

People reacting to each other is one factor which determines a general price level but thats not all. Not by a long shot. First, before you can even think of buying a stock, it has to be there for you to buy. How is a share of stock created? Why is it created? What is the process by which these shares get into your hands or the hands of investors like you? How many shares are outstanding? All these factors bear on the price you pay.

Once a stock is in your hands, where is it trading? Over-the-counter or on an exchange? On a national or regional exchange? The price making process, though similar in principle, does differ. This difference will have a bearing on the price you pay.

What does a specialist have to do with the price you pay? At times very much; at other times very little. It all depends. You should get some valuable insights here. What does a company have to do with the price of its stock? What does the S.E.C. have to do with the price of a stock? What does a broker have to do with the price of the stock you are buying or selling? All these things are important and they all interact to produce the prices you see. If you want to get the best price possible, you would do well to be aware of these factors.

Who are specialists? How are they chosen? What do they do? How do they make their money? Is the information on their book really as important as you have been led to believe? Are they really the villains everyone says they are? Let's find out.

What good are fundamentals in setting the price of a stock? What good are rumors? Charts? Emotions?

How do you enter an order?

What is a good market in a stock? A bad market? What happens to a stock in a bull market? In a bear market? These are all good questions.

Let's find out the answers. When you do, you'll not only have a pretty good idea of what determines the price you pay when you buy stock but you will also know how to go about getting the most favorable execution price.

The ideas and opinions expressed in this book are solely those of the author and his respondents and are not to be construed as in any way representative of those of the American Stock Exchange.

MICHAEL G. ZAHORCHAK
Linden, New Jersey

Contents

Favorable Executions

Wall Street's Most Cursed Men

EVERY industry and every society seems to have within its midst a category of workers or practitioners set apart from the rest of the group. Sometimes these people are loved, sometimes feared. Sometimes they are respected, despised, or joyously embraced while at other times they are treated like lepers, unclean persons to be avoided by the society at all costs.

Wall Street, too, has a similar group that commands just such attention. This group enjoys a unique position although currently it is in great danger of losing its favored status. The group is a small one. It varies at times from 550 to 600 members. This group working on the floors of the New York and American Stock Exchanges is known as the stock exchange specialists. They are at the same time feared, respected, held in awe, despised and more. They are accused of plotting and they are plotted against. Because of the power they appear to wield on the destiny of the companies whose stocks they trade as well as the nation's economy, some elements of our society would like nothing more than to drastically change the conditions under which these specialists do business.

As is so often the case, however, as the veil of ignorance surround-

1

ing the specialist is penetrated, one finds he is not the omnipotent person that the fictions, fantasies and attitudes fabricated over the years have led one to believe. These fictions have made the specialist not only the most misunderstood, but also the most cursed man on Wall Street. The pages which follow are designed to remove the various fictional and emotional garments clothing the specialist. This journey into the very core of the specialist system should prove fascinating to anyone interested enough in Wall Street who wants to learn how the securities business really works.

Much material published over the years has portrayed the exchanges as private clubs run stricly for the benefit of their members. Unfortunately, these allegations were true more often than not. Today, however, some of these charges are beginning to lose their validity. The reaction to the inequities exchange members have often created has been so great that the legislation now being proposed may leave the specialist with very little to say about how he will deploy his assets or what strategies he will use in the conduct of his business. Whether or not this will benefit or hurt investors, only time will tell.

Important changes in the specialist system as it relates to the Amex followed the scandals at the American Stock Exchange around 1960. The aftermath of these scandals not only gave teeth to the regulatory agencies but tremendously upgraded the quality of surveillance and self-regulation done by the Amex itself. At the same time, the markets have become increasingly institutionalized to the point where institutional customers began to use their economic muscle to force special favors from the exchange community. Concurrently the growth of the consumer movement focused increasing attention and emphasis on the need to protect the small shareholder.

Despite the securities laws; despite the growing, almost uncontrollable power of the mutual funds, pension funds and other institutions; despite the power of the corporations that originally issued the billions of shares of stock traded on the stock exchanges; despite everything, the myth continues to exist that the real economic power of the nation rests with the stock exchanges and that within the exchanges, with the specialists.

Over 80 per cent of the productive capacity of the nation plus large chunks of international capacity as well is represented in the shares traded on the two major national exchanges. Therefore, these allegations would be quite serious if they were substantially true.

Power of this enormity wherever lodged has no place in an enlightened society unless there are countervailing balances preventing its misuse. Hence, if power of this enormity does indeed rest in the hands of specialists, it too should be brought under control. But in the course of bringing this power under control, great care and restraint must be exercised to insure that the strengths and advantages of the auction transfer process are not sacrificed on the altar of change . . . or that the natural checks and balances of the auction process as it now exists are not destroyed merely to allow power to transfer to a new group.

The mere fact that stocks alternately move up, then down in price even though no substantive changes in operations have occurred, is not in and of itself any prima facie evidence of wrongdoing on the part of the specialist. This is true, even though the specialist assigned the stocks has profited as a result of these swings. In the stock market, as in everything else, the constant oscillation from one extreme to another is a normal, natural phenomenon. Therefore, unless a specialist himself has done something to deliberately influence investors, to give them an unwarranted illusion of confidence or disillusionment, he has not manipulated the market. In fact, he would be guilty of manipulation if he did not fairly permit the price of his stocks to reflect these changes both in real value and in psychological attitudes.

This, then, is what this book is all about. It's about the cursed men of Wall Street and how they affect you. It's about the auction markets; how they operate and how you can use them more advantageously. It's about the price you pay when you give your broker an order to buy stock, and the price you receive when you turn around to sell it. It's an in-depth study of the heart of the auction process as it exists today. With this knowledge you can judge for yourself the wisdom of the changes that are being proposed for tomorrow.

You will get to see just who specialists are, how they are selected, how they operate and what economic motivation exists to attract men into this business. You will get to see how they use the information on their books. You will see how the orders on the book affect you when you make a trade, how this affects the price of your stocks and how it stimulates the action the specialist takes.

You will get to know the specialist as a person. You will see how he thinks, acts and reacts. You will see how far he can go before having to account for his actions.

Looking over his shoulder you will see what he considers a good stock and a bad stock. You will see what he considers a healthy market and an unhealthy one. You will learn how a specialist might possibly help or hurt a market and how you can possibly use this information to your advantage.

Knowing how this most professional of all professionals thinks, you will learn how you too can go about improving your own investment results by seeing what happens to stocks during both bull and bear markets. Knowing what determines the price of a stock at any one time, you can learn to anticipate more precisely how the specialist and the market will react to any order you may place in the future. Knowing all this will provide the insights you need to go about the business of getting the most favorable executions possible under any and all circumstances.

2

You've Got to See It to Believe It

Among the prime New York City tourist attractions are the two stock exchanges. The visitor's gallery at the Amex is especially deceptive because nothing about it prepares the visitor for the excitement in store for him. Everything leading up to the view of the Exchange smacks of low key understatement. Even getting to the Amex causes time to stand still. The visitor is likely to get there by walking through the cemetery at Trinity Church where the frantic pace of lower Manhattan not merely stops but where time goes back several hundred years. Buried here are some of the earliest settlers of New York as well as leaders such as Alexander Hamilton and Robert Fulton.

As he comes through the revolving doors of the visitor's entrance on Trinity Place, the tone of understatement is maintained as the visitor steps on one of those swift, silent escalators that take him up several stories to the visitor's gallery. Here, waiting to greet him are attractive multilingual guides who lead him into a theater where a movie takes the visitor through 75 years of history in just a few minutes. At the end, the narration closes with an invitation of welcome to the visitor. He is greeted with: "Welcome—Welcome to the sights and sounds of the American Stock Exchange!" At this point the entire wall of the theater swiftly and silently slides open and the visitor is overpowered with the deafening roar of the activity on the trading floor below him.

Because everything up to this point has been so subdued, sophisticated, elegant and well-staged, even the visitor who has been forewarned of the planned chaos he will observe, is generally unprepared for the crescendo of noise this activity generates until he looks down from the gallery and sees it laid out beneath him.

Down below, on the Trading Floor the tides of fortune continually ebb and flow. Depending on the emotions that men allow to rule them, here is where their fortunes are capitalized and their empires toppled to be crumbled to dust. The organized confusion at the feet of the visitor is not just a put on, not just an act, not just a classroom assignment or a philosophical or semantical exercise. What he sees below him is the real thing. It is drama in the making.

On the Floor the visitor sees over a thousand people milling around with less apparent direction than an army of ants whose hill has just been disturbed. Everywhere people seem to be moving about with the speed of marathon walkers, not around a predetermined track but going off in every direction. Those men not running about seem to be grouped together in agitated clusters around the outer perimeters of about a dozen large circular counters.

Along two walls, in bleacherlike tiers, are men standing behind podia with telephone headsets fixed to their ears, shouting, screaming, gesturing to gain the attention of counterparts milling about the floor below them.

On each of the four walls, ticker tape screens incessantly flash a record of transactions taking place on the floor below. Thousands of numbers and letters race across the screen, each seemingly trying to out race the other during the few brief seconds of their existence before disappearing off the edge of the screen into oblivion.

Both ends of the room sparkle with red, white and green numbers on large lighted scoreboards several stories high flashing to gain the attention of brokers busily going about their business.

For many people, all this is heady stuff. Because of the excitement generated here, many people look to become part of this thing; this stock market on the minds and tongues of 31 million investors, which so vitally affects the economic well-being of millions more.

It is inevitable that some who come here will be disappointed.

Though perhaps it is better to have tasted the excitement of this arena and gone away unsatisfied than not to have known such excitement could exist.

One person who probably would strongly disagree with this statement is Don Smith, chairman of Wolverine-Pentronix, a company that listed about 10 years ago. He came to the Exchange to take part in the ceremonies that coincide with the start of trading of any new stock. What he saw overwhelmed him as it does most people. However, instead of being exhilarated by what he saw, he was appalled; so much so that he went straight home to write a highly critical letter of his observations to his shareholders.

In it he observed that "The screaming and shouting. . . . sounded like bedlam coming from the Floor of the Exchange. More like a fish market than a sedate place of business. . . . We watched the activity on the Floor . . . it looked like a bunch of grownups playing cowboys and Indians."

His letter went on to allege manipulation by the specialist because his stock closed lower that afternoon than it opened. He alleged that this was done deliberately by his specialist so that he could make $12.50 on the stock Mr. Smith purchased from him earlier in the day to officially open the trading in Wolverine stock.

Unfortunately, this man did not understand the process by which investment intentions are translated into investment values, and apparently, no one he talked to at the time was able to explain it to his satisfaction. As a result, needless animosity was created, and he felt compelled to withdraw or delist his stock from Amex trading.

In the chapters which follow, the reader will have an opportunity to gain insights into the mechanics of the auction process in a manner which our disillusioned friend was never privileged to see. We will go down from the gallery directly to the Floor of the Exchange itself were Larry Harkins, a hypothetical specialist will let us observe him in action.

How It All Began

BEFORE we go down to meet Larry, it might be well to review the history of stock markets as we know it to be.

Anyone, like our friend who listed the shares of his company and then immediately moved to delist them, who steps onto the Floor of the Exchange to be confronted with the screaming and shouting of the place has actually succeeded in his first impression to capture the essence, the flavor, the charisma, the excitement of the market place precisely. This is what it is all about. A viable, active, successful auction is nothing if it is not like bedlam. It is the interaction of buyer and seller, each attempting to gain an advantage over the other that sets up the emotional interplay that appears so much like bedlam.

But if all one sees are the negative aspects of this activity he has failed to perceive clearly what all auction markets since the dawn of civilization have been. The only thing that makes the auction market on the American Stock Exchange different than the one at the Parke-Bernet Galleries in midtown Manhattan is that the merchandise being traded differs.

Nevertheless, all auction markets have been arenas where emotions

8

and the excitement of the moment have swayed the participants, as they have frantically sought to outbid each other for limited quantities of what they considered to be valuable merchandise; or conversely at other times as multiple sellers have tried all sorts of competitive stratagems to move their goods on to disinterested buyers with limited wants.

Whether the auction market deals in securities, art objects, produce, commodities, fish, harem girls, slaves or tulips, the principles remain the same. All active auction markets generate noise as people compete with each other in acquiring or disposing of their merchandise.

Actually, the American Stock Exchange appears more confused and agitated than it really is because of the nature of its organization. The Amex is not just one auction market, but as many as 165 separate auction markets being conducted simultaneously. Furthermore, these 165 markets are so constructed that both buyers and sellers are simultaneously competing with other buyers and sellers and with each other. Even the Parke-Bernet Galleries, one of the most prestigious auctions in the world, would generate considerable activity and confusion if they attempted to conduct 165 separate sales of art objects all at the same time while sellers of other art objects were attempting to persuade the auctioneers to place their pieces on the auction blocks next. Not only would the activity arise from the interaction of the sellers and the auctioneer, but also by the buyers themselves as they rushed from one sale to the next in an effort not to miss an opportunity to bid on all the items they wanted to buy.

The significant error in criticizing this sort of activity comes from having a preconception of the format which an auction market "should" have. The objective is not form but substance. So far the most efficient means devised to expeditiously transfer many commodities has been through the screaming, shouting format of the auction process. Anyone who disagrees obviously has not studied his history. To have done so would have shown that every time freely fluctuating markets have operated where the value of the merchandise being traded has been set on a competitive, continuous, two-way auction basis, they have always appeared, to the uninitiated casual observer to be scenes of raving, uncontrollable confusion rather than the exceedingly sensitive, responsive mechanisms they have invariably proved to be.

The important thing to remember, and something that is often overlooked is the fact that despite all the noise and seeming confusion, a market such as the Amex is nevertheless efficient, and closely regulated.

On the Amex, every trade that takes place is recorded and electronically monitored to insure that the auction process works effectively. When questionable trades are discovered they are quickly brought to the staff's attention.

Getting back to the origins of the stock market, no one quite knows when or where the first stock exchange was located. Some believe it may have been with the Phoenicians in pre-Christian times. Certainly they employed auctions, both to accumulate and to dispose of the merchandise they traded. Others have even claimed that a market mechanism remarkably similar to our present day stock markets was described in Chinese writings believed to be as much as 4,000 years old.

Be that as it may, the first stock market we are sure of was described in a book by Joseph de la Vega writen in 1688. To that gentleman goes the honor of launching the first of what has become a torrential flood of stock market books. Interestingly, like so many other initial ventures, this remains a classic in its field. It is one of the best stock market books ever written.

The name of his book, translated into English, is *Confusion of Confusions*. It describes the Amsterdam stock market of the mid-seventeenth century, and it is outstanding because even then, de la Vega was perceptive enough to recognize the dual nature of almost everything connected with the market.

Thus, while one group of people may be pleased about the rise in the price of a stock, another group who earlier had sold out, or those waiting to buy at lower prices, are perturbed. Then, while those who purchase stocks at high prices are distressed by a drop in the price of a stock, those waiting to buy stand to benefit from the decline. Although a manipulator might defraud and cause damage to a specific individual, his manipulative activities, if successful, might benefit numerous other shareholders.

Even in 1688, this pioneer stock market book captured the spirit of the auction market bedlam when it described the activity on the Amsterdam Exchange as the greatest comedy in the magnificent theater of the world. To de la Vega, the market was a place where speculators excelled in tricks finding excuses for the ". . . concealment of facts, quarrels, provocations, mockery, idle talk, violent desires, collusion, artful deceptions, betrayals, cheatings, and (where) even the tragic and the comic (are) to be found." To read this, it is obvious that nothing half so exciting occurs on the stock markets of today because everyone today seems to take this whole game so unbelievably seriously.

De la Vega found the conduct of business on the Exchange to be as ridiculous as the game itself. In order to transact business it was first necessary to find a buyer or seller willing to trade. Then it was necessary to take his hand and shake it as a sign of your willingness to do business with him. These were no ordinary handshakes, however, but a form of overt aggression which caused the hands of active traders to swell several glove sizes by the end of each day.

After a short interval of trading ". . . the hands redden from the blows (I believe from the shame that even the most respected people do business in such an indecent manner as with blows). The handshakes are followed by shouting, the shouting by insults, the insults by impudence and more insults, shouting, pushes, and handshakes until the business is finished. . . . Some applaude the cheating . . . as at a comedy . . . clapping their hands together."

It is obvious from this description that market practices have advanced considerably since those beginning days. The shouting and apparent confusion remain, but the physical violence is gone as well as the open and anticipated cheating. Today a person who attempts to use the market improperly is the exception rather than the rule, with regulatory bodies of all kinds going to considerable expense to insure, so far as possible, that the integrity of the market place is maintained.

For those interested in the full text of this fascinating work, it is available from the Kress Business Library and published by the Harvard University Press.

4

The Markets of Today

IN THE 1600s the institution known as the stock market was exclusive with the Dutch, particularly with the citizens of Amsterdam, where the market became a dominant factor in their life-style. Not only was there a viable organized stock exchange in Amsterdam by 1688 where trading took place each afternoon, but there were equally active open air curb markets on Wormaestreet and in the "church square" where people could trade stocks mornings and on Sundays when the Exchange itself was closed. Actually there is nothing we have in the way of markets in this country today that did not exist in Holland hundreds of years ago.

As international trade first with China and the East Indies, then with the New World expanded, businessmen in the coastal countries of Europe organized the joint ventures needed to provide the capital for this trade. To transfer the ownership shares of those early ventures and later of the companies that pioneered in the development of the industrial revolution, stock exchanges were begun. They spread from Holland to England and France, then to other countries throughout the world.

It is interesting to note that not even Russia, who has been such a vociferous foe of the capitalistic system was spared the prestige of its own national stock exchange. By 1859 the Russians had a stock exchange operating in full swing in an exquisitely beautiful building in St. Petersburg or Leningrad, as it has been called since 1924. The building, which now houses the Central Navy Museum was located at a point on Vasiyevsky Island directly across the river from the Czar's Imperial Palace, which is now world renowned as the Hermitage museum.

Today, most of the world's trading in stock occurs on just four stock exchanges. When it comes to volume of trading, the biggest stock exchange by far is the Tokyo Stock Exchange. Next with occasional high volume bursts is the Toronto Stock Exchange, although generally its volume is below that of the New York Stock Exchange.

In terms of monetary value of shares traded, however, the New York Stock Exchange ranks first with the American Stock Exchange second.

The Japanese, with their inimitable ability to miniaturize everything, took the stock market concept and merchandised it with a vengeance. Where 100 shares is generally a round lot in this country, it is 1,000 shares in Japan.

While the small investor here might think of buying only 5 or 10 shares of a low priced stock, in Japan, there are literally hundreds of stocks that can be purchased in 100 share odd lots for under $5 per hundred shares. In this country the minimum stock exchange commission is more than that!

Millions of investors in Japan invest as little as $3 per month in heavily promoted monthly investment plans. Except for the highest priced blue chips such as the Sony Coorporation, which sometimes trades for $10 or more, most other stocks go for about 15 to 25 cents per share while lower quality stocks sell proportionately lower. It is no wonder then that these low prices combined with the Japanese total absorption in whatever they pursue has resulted in trading volume of over 100 million shares per day.

If the sensibilities of an American company president can be so easily bruised by the bedlam of activity on the relatively sedate American Stock Exchange, a visit to the Floor of the Tokyo Stock Exchange will undoubtedly convince the visitor that he surely has entered into the mouth of Dante's *Inferno* from which there is not the slightest hope of escape.

The Toronto Stock Exchange derives occasional volume bursts because the majority of the issues traded on that Exchange are mineral exploration companies. Many are low priced, highly speculative stocks with large amounts of outstanding shares. Because of their low price, they often are referred to as crap shooting stocks. That is, regardless of their apparent lack of value, someone almost always seems willing to trade them, not on an investment basis but on the chance that the company might someday discover significant commercial mineralization on its properties. Whenever this happens or when just the rumor of a possible find reaches the market, trading picks up not only in the stock involved but in stocks of all the other companies in the vicinity of the rumored discovery.

Despite the record volume of trading that occurs regularly on the Tokyo Stock Exchange, the king of stock exchanges is the New York Stock Exchange. The N.Y.S.E. pre-eminence is achieved by the fact that the 1,900 odd corporations listed on the Exchange account for almost 70 per cent of the total net income earned by all U.S. corporations. These same companies control over 30 per cent of all the nation's corporate assets and account for 37 per cent of all corporate sales and revenues according to figures compiled by that Exchange.

Several blocks away, on the American Stock Exchange, about 1,500 different securities issued by over 1,200 companies are listed. These securities represent an aggregate market value of over $60 billion. As huge as this amount seems, it is, nevertheless, small compared to the assets represented on the New York Stock Exchange.

In addition to these two exchanges, there are 12 other exchanges in the United States. They are primarily concentrated on the east coast, in Boston, New York (National Stock Exchange), Philadelphia-Baltimore-Washington, and Pittsburgh; in the midwest, in Chicago (Chicago Board of Trade and the Midwest Stock Exchange), Cincinnati and Detroit; and in the far west, in Los Angeles and San Francisco (Pacific Coast Exchange), Salt Lake City and Spokane. All of these exchanges are registered with and supervised by the Securities and Exchange Commission. There is one other regional exchange in Honolulu which is exempt from S.E.C. registration. In Canada, most major cities in addition to Toronto have stock exchanges including Montreal, Calgary, Winnipeg and Vancouver.

Elsewhere throughout the world, stock exchanges are located in Argentina, Belgium, Brazil, France, Germany, Great Britain, Hong Kong, Italy, Mexico, the Netherlands, Switzerland, Sweden and South Africa. In addition, despite all the talk of Communist encroachment in the underdeveloped nations of the world, the founding of several more stock exchanges seems to be a distinct possibility. In the past few years the U.S. exchanges have been regularly visited by representatives from other nations, including Pakistan, Taiwan and Iran, looking to either start exchanges in their countries or improve on the framework of securities trading that already exists in those countries.

Although there are these stocks exchanges throughout the world, a person who was familiar with the operations of one exchange would not necessarily know how the others operate because the trading of securities throughout the world is conducted in four broadly different ways.

The Americans are most familiar with the markets of the Amex and the N.Y.S.E. These are characterized as continuous two-way auction markets. An auction market is one where prices are not fixed but instead are determined competitively either by buyers who compete with each other to buy an article from one seller or by sellers who seek to attract potential buyers to their wares.

A two-way auction implies that at the same time that buyers are competing with each other to buy a commodity, sellers are also competing with each other to sell that same commodity. It is the interaction of these two groups alternately pushing prices up by their bids on one hand and down by their offers on the other that causes prices to fluctuate.

In addition, the auction is continuous because unfilled bids and offers are not wiped off the books after each trade but remain to become factors in all future transactions until the orders are either filled or cancelled.

The supervisor of this auction process on American stock exchanges is a man known as the specialist. It is the specialist to whom orders to buy and sell stocks either at the best available current price or at specified prices are relayed. The specialist guarantees to hold orders entered at fixed prices for brokers and execute them on the broker's behalf if and when the stock should trade at the specified price provided only that all orders at the same price that were earlier left with the specialist be executed first.

A characteristic of this continuous auction market is that about 85 per cent of the time, the person buying a stock does so directly (through his agent) from a selling investor without the stock first going into the inventory of a dealer or some other middleman who extracts a markup for having held the stock in his inventory.

Other characteristics are a continuity in price from one trade to the next with each successive price bearing a direct relationship to the preceding trade price. For example, successive transactions of a stock might be priced as follows: 40; 40⅛; 40⅜; 40¼; 40⅜ In contrast, a discontinuous pricing structure would be 40; 42; 37; 35; 41, etc. This continuity occurs because the specialist is obligated to absorb into an inventory he personally maintains or to release from this inventory, sufficient stock to offset market pressures whenever existing public orders are insufficient to provide this price continuity.

This in turn insures that anyone who insists on buying or selling a stock immediately without regard to price will always find someone available to buy stock from or sell it to. This investor knows that with the specialist filling in the price gaps the price will be the best available price at any particular moment in time.

In contrast to a two-way auction market supervised by a specialist is a two-way auction market where no specialist is responsible for maintaining price continuity. The auction market as it operates on the Toronto Stock Exchange is an example of this. It appears that while no specialists are specifically assigned to any stock, one or more floor traders usually take it upon themselves to make a market in a stock. These floor traders usually perform some of the functions of American specialists. However, since they perform voluntarily their conduct is not governed by the Exchange. Therefore, they are free to refuse to trade with the public or with any particular broker for whatever reason, whenever they choose to do so.

On a Toronto type of market for example a broker with an order to buy stock at $20 must contend with more variables than his United States counterpart. First he would probably take his order to the post where the stock is quoted. There a clerk maintains an open order book of all limit orders that have been left with him waiting to be executed. The clerk will quote the market to the broker based on the best prices shown on his book. This market might be as close as 19⅞–20 for instance or it might be as wide as 18–23.

By way of illustration assume the best bid on the book is 19¾ while the lowest offering price is 20½. The broker who wants to buy 100 shares at 20, now has two choices. He can either leave his order with the clerk, thus changing the quote on the book to 20–20½ or he might try to locate one of the floor traders making a market in the stock to see if the floor trader is willing to sell 100 shares at 20. If the floor trader wishes to lighten his inventory or go short, he might sell

100 shares to the broker. Otherwise, the broker has to go back to the post and leave his order with the clerk.

The problem with leaving an order with the clerk is that the broker has no guarantee that the order will be filled if the stock should sell at, or below 20. As peculiar as this might seem, numerous Canadians have said that stocks regularly trade on their exchanges at prices lower than orders they have given to their brokers. They claim orders left with the clerks are regularly overlooked even when their prices are more favorable than those at which trades are taking place.

The reason often given is that when a flurry of activity develops in a stock and a crowd congregates, brokers will trade directly with each other, ignoring orders left with the clerk because there is no obligation to give orders left with the clerk any priority consideration.

Therefore, it becomes the responsibility of the broker who left the order at the post to get it back from the clerk and attempt to execute it himself. If he is unsuccessful and again takes his order to the post, he may lose his favored position on the book. Often, when such flurries develop, the customer is advised that the broker was busy with other orders, and therefore could not get into the crowd in time to fill the order.

Situations of this kind are reported to be fairly common occurrences on auction markets not supervised by specialists specifically assigned to individual stocks.

Somewhat related to the Canadian style of auction market is the broker-dealer system exemplified by the over-the-counter market in this country. Under the broker-dealer system a broker announces that he is a dealer in certain stocks. He then "quotes" these stocks either in a publication popularly called the "pink sheets" or over an electronic quotation system known as NASDAQ.

Thereafter any other broker whose customer gives him an order to buy or sell the stock in question tries to find the dealer offering the best "quote."

When a stock is actively traded it often attracts many dealers who by competing are able to provide quotes with narrow spreads. On the other hand, during bear markets or when a stock is inactively traded, it is possible for a stock to be abandoned thus making it impossible for investors to trade the stock at any price.

The primary characteristics of a broker-dealer system therefore are the variability of broker interest and the fact that an investor rarely, if ever trades directly with another investor. Instead he trades with a dealer who either sells stock out of his inventory or who buys stock to add to his inventory.

In Europe, there is still another type of market known as the "Call Market." On call markets, stocks are traded one at a time. Demand is estimated and, on the basis of this estimate a price is set for each stock. All stocks are announced either alphabetically or in some other order, and all the prices announced. Anyone who either wants to buy or to sell can have his order executed at the call price for as long as it takes the clerks to match up all orders on the books. As soon as all orders at this call price have been entered, the books are closed until the next call. The next stock in line is called, its trading price announced and so on down the list. Each stock might be called twice a day and brokers are free either to accept or to reject the call price but they are not free to enter counter proposals. If they reject a call, however, they cannot do business in the stock until the next time it is called because there is no continuity in the trading process.

Most securities business in Europe is transacted through banks rather than brokerage houses. Therefore, it is the bankers who determine the call prices based on the orders and inventories they have on hand just prior to the call. The basis of each call price is the figure which they estimate will be attractive enough to appropriately offset actual orders they have on hand. It is obvious that a call market is a cumbersome, inexact kind of market, not at all suited to handle transactions of large numbers of stocks in large quantities with a large number of stockholders. For these reasons, representatives of many European exchanges have been observing the practices and procedures in American markets in order to determine how best to adapt their markets to the changing times even as we are under pressure to change our markets to something that may end up being less flexible than the present system.

5

The View From the Floor

THE FIRST thing a visitor notices as he steps onto the trading floor on his way to Larry's post is the drop in the noise level as compared to the noise in the visitor's gallery. This is probably because the gallery gets the noise both as it rises from the floor, and then again when it bounces down from the roof.

The next thing he becomes aware of are the people. From the visitor's gallery, the people on the trading floor appear to be rushing around aimlessly. But despite their haste, no one appears to collide with anyone else.

You soon discover as you are almost knocked over, that whatever they have to keep from colliding, you don't.

You are led right smack to the middle of the floor; to post number seven to watch Larry Harkins in action. There is a crowd milling about Larry when you get to the post so there is no way for you to get to him at the moment. While waiting for the crowd to break up, however, you have an opportunity to examine the Exchange from a new vantage point. From the center of the floor, the room seems even bigger than it did from the gallery above. From the middle of the floor, the two ends of the Exchange seem to be an infinity away.

Although the Exchange is becoming increasingly automated, the current physical layout speaks eloquently of the Exchange's history as an outdoor curb market. When they were outside, both brokers and clerks became accustomed to communicating with each other by shouting and hand signalling back and forth; from the broker on the street to his clerk on the second story window ledges. It seemed natural therefore when the indoor exchange was constructed, to perpetuate this practice. The floor plan of the Exchange thus is vivid testimony to the concept that while brokers themselves deal with prices that are in a constant state of change, their own work patterns, once acquired are calcified permitting changes to evolve only with the greatest effort.

To perpetuate the relative position of the broker and his clerk, the indoor market succeeded in positioning the clerks above the eye level of the broker by building banks of bleacherlike tiers along the entire length of the granite-faced room. Set in neat rows on these tiers are boxes, much like box seats in a sports arena, thereby enhancing the illusion that the Exchange floor is not so much a place of business as it is a stadium in which is played daily some sort of spectacular human extravaganza.

From these indoor bleachers they could continue to signal down to the floor, using their same hand signals and shuts creating a discordant chorus that even the most rabid sports fans could never hope to duplicate.

Each exchange member who functions as a broker has to have at least one clerk stationed at a booth assigned to him to receive, relay and transmit orders or other instructions back and forth between himself and his partners or the registered representatives in his office.

On the floor itself there are 11 large circular counter arrangements called trading posts. Post number seven where Larry conducts his business is one of these eleven.

Each stock listed on the Exchange is assigned to a specific specialist unit who in turn is permitted to do business only at a specific area at one of these posts. Even the post itself is a throwback to the days when stocks were traded on the street, although the counter arrangements in use today bear no resemblance to anything like the post of old.

Going back to the time of the curbside markets, trading in specific stocks eventually tended to take place at certain identifiable spots in the street. Brokers who wanted to trade any particular stock always knew where they might find other brokers interested in trading the same stock.

For convenience sake, each stock had a specific location where people interested in trading it would be found. Eventually, one broker in each location became the "specialist" in trading the stock. This practice is carried on even to this day.

It was only natural then, though perhaps "corny" as we look back in time, that when brokers first moved indoors they chose lampposts as the symbol of the fixed location where stocks were to be traded. As a matter of fact, actual lampposts were originally installed in orderly rows on the Trading Floor around which brokers wishing to trade stocks could congregate.

Around the circumference of the post, each specialist is assigned a segment about four feet wide where he conducts his business. During business hours the specialist or one of his partners is always within a few feet of this assigned location.

Besides the specialist, a number of other people work at each post. Some of them work directly for the specialist while others are employed by the Exchange. Each specialist has working for him, one or more clerks who help him with his paper work.

Several exchange employees known as reporters are also assigned to each post to officially record each stock transaction as it takes place. Every broker who sells stock is obligated to report the sale to a reporter at the post. The reporter mark senses the official entry of each trade on a computer card which he passes along to one of the employees working inside the post.

Inside the post, are operators who transmit the details of each trade on to the system that feeds it to the ticker tapes and information consoles in operation throughout the world.

Considering that the average specialist may trade 50,000 or more shares of his busiest stocks on a typical day, the record keeping systems on the Exchange Floor appear unbelievably casual to the outside observer. Yet the system has held up well under all the stresses that have been placed on it even as transfer agents, back offices and others became hopelessly bogged down in the paper work jams of the late 1960s. During the entire period, Exchange floor operations managed to function efficiently, using nothing more to record transactions totaling billions of dollars than small scraps of paper no bigger in size than 3 by 4 inches.

When one realizes that as many as 20,000 to 40,000 separate trades take place on an average day, each of which generates at least 2 or 3 pieces of paper, it is remarkable both that so few papers get lost and that the system has proved to so efficient.

The People of the Exchange

ONCE A visitor has oriented himself to the physical layout of the trading floor, his next question usually has to do with the people milling about the place.

He sees people on the tiers along both sides of the Trading Floor, some writing on pads, some speaking into the telephone, some shouting to people on the Floor. At floor level, he sees people scurrying about while others are leaning on the counters of the posts apparently doing nothing. At some spots on the Floor, there are groups of people crowding around trying to jostle their way into the center of the crowd while others are breaking away from them, gesturing madly as they move.

Some people are dressed in business suits while others are wearing tan or blue poplin jackets. The visitor notices that everyone has a badge but the badges are different. Even the visitor himself had to be identified and given a badge before being permitted on the Trading Floor. Some badges contain pictures identifying their owners, while other have identifying names and numbers on them.

The visitor naturally enough wants to know who all these people are and what they are doing. He learns that there are three broad categories of people engaged in the drama of the Exchange. One group consists of those people who are the members of the Exchange while the other two groups are employees either of the members or of the Exchange itself. The larger group of employees works directly for and is paid by members, while a smaller group consists of people employed by the Exchange to insure that Floor operations run smoothly.

The American Stock Exchange has 650 members. Except for a few memberships occasionally held in the estates of former members virtually all memberships are active. Each membership is issued in the name of an individual even though a brokerage house may have paid for or otherwise controls the membership.

In order to become a member of the Exchange, a person first has to find an existing member looking to sell his "seat." They must then mutually agree with each other as to the price and terms of payment. After this is done, but before the seat actually changes hands, the prospective member must apply for membership. A member is subject to a rather thorough character investigation after which he is given an examination to determine that he knows the rules for transacting business on the Floor. Having passed this requirement, his membership is put up for a vote by the Board of Governors. Invariably, if a candidate's record is clean, he will get the Board's approval.

Up to now people have bought memberships because of the money they thought they could make by being members of the exchange. Therefore, the price of a seat varied at any time by the projected profitability to the member and how much he is willing to pay to achieve this profitability.

Most members fall into two broad categories, brokers and specialists. Brokers buy memberships because of the money they think they will generate in commissions by buying and selling stocks for their customers, while specialists buy memberships because they think they have the ability to "make markets in stocks" in a manner that will satisfy Exchange rules and at the same time prove profitable to themselves.

The cost of membership over the years has varied enormously from $650 in 1942 to $350,000 in 1969. Generally, as daily trading volume increases, the price of a seat goes up. Conversely, when trading volume dries up or when challenges face the industry, people become less willing to enter the business, causing the price of seats to drop.

The profit of a membership to a broker stems from the fact that people trading in stocks have in the past paid their broker a standard, fixed "minimum" commission on all their orders. Brokers on the other hand pay no commissions to the Exchange except for a transactions fee that comes to about one per cent of the commission they charge their customers. Recently the question of commissions has become cloudy throwing the future profitability of the business into some confusion. At this writing a fixed commission is in effect on all orders up to $300,000 with the commission on that part of an order over $300,000 up for negotiation. The level at which negotiation is to begin is scheduled to drop soon to $100,000. Further pressure is being brought to bear to eliminate the fixed commission entirely and open up orders of all sizes to competitive negotiation.

Of the Exchange's 650 members, about 475 are brokers while most of the rest are those cursed people of Wall Street, the specialists.

Exchange employees on the Floor range from those who interpret operating rules and settle disputes between members to clerical personnel. Among the latter are reporters, who, as we saw, record every trade that takes place as to time, quantity and price. In turn they give this information to operators of the transmitting machines who enter the data on computers which service the ticker tapes and information storage systems.

It is important to keep in mind that stock exchange members do not work for the Exchange. Technically, it is the other way around. The stock exchange is an association owned by its 650 members. However, the exchanges have come under increasing control of the S.E.C. and other regulatory agencies. Until now, at least so far as the Amex specialist is concerned, he is in essence a journeyman employee who operates a business on the Exchange Floor. Instead of being on the payroll of the Exchange or on the payroll of those who are regulating him, however, he must provide his own capital.

Although the members technically own the Exchange, since the reorganization of the Amex as a result of the scandals that rocked the exchange in 1961, a staff was created which has been functioning independently, almost autonomously from the membership insofar as supervising, regulating and disciplining them is concerned. The staff has been operating more and more as though it were a semi-regulatory agency of the government.

We noted that the membership composition of the Exchange fell into two broad categories, brokers and specialists. In the broker category, there are several subgroupings.

First and foremost is the commission broker. He represents about

60 per cent or 400 of all Amex members. Commission brokers are partners or stockholders in the brokerage houses which do business with what the brokerage community euphemistically calls "the general public." Any time a customer of one of these brokers puts in an order to buy or sell stock, that order is relayed by phone or wire to the firm's commission broker on the Exchange Floor who takes it to the appropriate specialist for execution. The primary function of a commission broker is to execute his firm's orders on the best possible terms according to the specific instructions of the customer. All orders from customers who are not members of an exchange are called public orders whether they are for an odd lot of ten shares or a controlling block of several hundred thousand shares.

In addition to commission brokers and specialists, the remaining Amex members work for others as "Floor Brokers" or for themselves as "Registered Traders." Quite often members perform both these functions interchangeably. Floor brokers are also known as "Two-Dollar Brokers." They often own their own memberships independently of any affiliation with a member firm. Their work consists of freelancing for member firms when the firm's own broker is ill, on vacation or just too busy to handle all the orders his firm is generating.

Often two-dollar brokers are unusually competent at handling difficult orders such as those involving the purchase or sale of a large block of stock over an extended period of time. When some firms get such orders or at the insistence of customers for whatever their personal reasons, they may farm out such orders to a competent two-dollar broker.

These brokers are so named because originally they received $2 per hundred shares on each order they executed. Now, however, the amount of money they receive varies between about $1 and $5 per round lot depending on the selling price of the stock.

The registered trader is what the name implies. He is what the market used to be all about. Like a two-dollar broker, he has no affiliation with anyone else. Some may not even rent themselves out as two-dollar brokers. All they do is come to the Floor each day to trade stocks for their own accounts.

These are the people who in the "good old days" were accused along with the specialists and the pool operators of conducting the bull and bear raids we now read so much about. In recent years, however, so many rules and restrictions have been placed on these men that now their impact on the market is quite minimal. They are regulated at least as closely as the specialist and, like him, can only do their trading in ways that tend to stabilize the market.

As a result they can no longer "play games" with stocks. Now the only way they can trade profitably is to know the market significantly better than the average trader off the Exchange, then use this knowledge plus their proximity to the action to get in and out of stocks quickly. Because of the restrictions placed on them, the price of a membership seems too high for the return that they can expect to get from it. As a result, the number of registered traders along with the percentage of over-all trading they account for has been declining in recent years to the point where recently their trading accounts for a small fraction of one per cent of total Exchange volume.

On the New York Stock Exchange, there is one additional class of member not found on the Amex. This is the member known as the "odd-lot" dealer. Odd lot dealers handle the orders that come in for less than 100 shares of those stocks which normally trade in units or round lots of 100 shares. At every post on the N.Y.S.E. there is a member who is affiliated with an "Odd-Lot" house. On the Amex, however, the specialist in a stock is also the odd-lot dealer.

The Amex practice dates back to the times when daily volume was measured in hundred thousand share rather than million share daily totals, and the specalists needed all the income sources they could find. It was decided at that time that specialists would handle their own odd lots. Since that time, although volume has increased tremendously, so has the specialists capacity to handle this volume. Consequently, the practice of handling odd lots by specialists continues to this day.

With all this background a visitor is now in a good position to understand the idea behind all the apparent confusion he sees all around him. All he has to do is to imagine the trading Floor of the Amex as being nothing more than a big barn in which a sophisticated version of a farmer's auction takes place every day. Instead of just one auctioneer, however, who puts up merchandise to sell one item at a time to the highest bidder, there are at least 160 auctioneers, each stationed at a predetermined fixed spot on the Floor of the barn. Each of these auctioneers is conducting his own separate independent auction at the same time as all the other auctioneers. However, each auctioneer does not just conduct one auction at a time. Instead he is simultaneously conducting auctions in 8 stocks on average, both buying and selling each stock at the same time.

Each specialist stands pat at his post conducting his auction in those stocks assigned to him while the floor brokers hurry about from one post to another then back to the tiers along the sides in the process of executing orders to buy and sell stocks at these auctions. They move about going from one auction location to the other according to the instructions they receive.

7

Managing the Crowd

THE CROWD milled about Larry's post for well over an hour before a semblance of order came to the post.

Watching him handle the crowd was like watching a composer conduct a symphony. As brokers alternately came into and left the crowd, Larry would first create a crescendo of excitement by drawing brokers from the crowd toward him. Then, having achieved the tonal effect he desired, he would still the crowd and wave them back until he was ready for the next movement of his symphony to begin.

Throughout the morning brokers came and went. Sometimes singly, sometimes converging in groups of three or four. Always there were at least four brokers standing nearby waiting for an opportunity to sell large blocks of stock. Many who came also had orders to buy but most of the brokers who stopped did so out of curiosity just as people do any time there is a fire, an accident or anything else that attracts their attention.

They would stop a few moments, observe the action, then go about their business. The brokers interested in trading would stay a little longer. Some, after observing the activity would turn toward the side lines screaming and hand signaling information back to their offices. All this organized confusion gave the area around the post the appearance of a caucas room at a deaf-mutes' convention during a heated debate.

Every time someone new came to the post, the crowd surged forward to hear what he had to say.

"How's ZAP?"

"42, a quarter."

"Buy a thousand at an eighth."

"You got it!" screamed four brokers from the crowd in unison. "Your seller is Windsor," says Larry pointing to one of the four while waving the other three back.

Another man rushes in "ZAP?"

"42–¼"

"Sell a hundred at the market."

"O.K. Clear Higgins, Smith."

Larry reaches into a cubbyhole under the counter of his post for a handful of tickets. The ticket on top reads, "Buy 5000 ZAP 42." The name on the ticket reads Higgins, Smith & Co. The 5,000 had been scratched off. The most recent entry is "32" which Larry scratches out to replace with "31."

What this tells him is that of an original order left with him to buy 5,000 shares of ZAP at 42, he has succeeded in buying 1,900 shares leaving 3,100 shares still to be purchased. At the same time, on the bottom of the ticket he writes "1–461." This shorthand will tell Higgins, Smith & Co. that the seller of this latest 100 shares was a broker whose clearing house number is 461.

"How's ZAP?"

"42–¼."

The broker snaps "I've got stock to sell at an eighth." There is no response from the crowd so he hands Larry a ticket which reads "Sell 3,000 ZAP 42⅛." Larry reaches for his open orders and puts the ticket right on top of his sell orders. He looks up and shouts to the crowd. "New quote. The market is now 42–⅛."

"Size. Size. What's the size?"

"Thirty one hundred by three thousand."

Everyone in the crowd turns in the direction of their floor clerks shouting and signaling madly. Each broker is telling his clerk that the offer has been lowered to 42⅛ with 3,000 to sell at that price.

Each broker is signalling to ask for further instructions. The Brown Brothers broker gets his instructions first. He is to stand pat, offering stock only when bids appear.

Zimmerman is next. His orders are to sell at market before anyone else steps in ahead of him. He confirms this and whirls around to face the specialist. "Sell 3,100 ZAP at 42. Sell 1,600 ZAP at market."

"You got it. 3,100 at 42; 1,600 at 41⅞. My clerk will give you the names. The new quote is 41¾–42⅛."

Zimmerman entered his order the way he did to prevent Larry from buying the entire block at 41⅞. Under the rules Larry is supposed to get his customers the best price possible. This means that even though a customer is willing to buy stock for 42, if he can buy the stock for the customer at a lower price he is obligated to do so. In practice this would never happen so long as Larry had an order to sell small lots of stock at 42. But when faced with an order like Zimmerman's to sell more than 3,100 shares, the specialist either has to buy the remaining 1,600 himself at 42 or he has to allow the price to drop down to the next level of bids on his book. When he does this, and if the next level is down just ⅛ point as it was in this case, the specialist may, at his discretion, price the entire block at 41⅞ rather than break it up into two separate trades.

This benefits the buyer at 42 of course because he saves an ⅛ point on his order but it works against the seller who gets an ⅛ point less than he might otherwise have received on at least part of his order. The Zimmerman broker being market wise decided to take no chances. His obligation was to get the best price for his customer. Knowing the size of the bid at 42 was 3,100 shares, he offered to sell 3,100 at 42. This would exactly offset the orders on the book. Then he offered just the remaining 1,600 shares at the market. By this device he assured his customer the best average price possible for his block regardless of what he received for the remaining 1,600 shares.

"500 at the market" says a voice excitedly.

"500 what, you dummy!"

"Sorry about that. 500 to sell at the market."

"You got it at ¾. The market is still 41¾–⅛."

"Sell another 500 at market."

"O.K., the market's still ¾–⅛."

"How much more will go at ¾?"

"1,800."

"O.K. Sold."

"The market's now 41⅝–42"

"41⅝ for how many?"

"4,600."

"Make it 5,200 at ⅝."

"Only if it cleans up your order. Otherwise its ⅜ on the remaining 600 shares."

"Fair enough. 5,200 cleans me up. I won't be back."

In this brief interchange, Windsor has just sold 8,000 shares at the market. He first sold 2,800 shares at 41¾ in three successive trades of 500, 500 and 1,800 shares. Then he sold the remaining 5,200 shares at 41⅝. The specialist had orders to buy only 4,600 shares at 41⅝ when Windsor countered with his offer to sell 5,200 shares at that price. Larry then agreed to buy the remaining 600 shares for his own account, but only if he received assurances that this would "clean up" or complete the order. When Windsor gave him this assurance, Larry bought the remaining 600 shares for his own account.

If Windsor & Co. had more stock to sell, Larry would have matched the remaining 600 shares against orders he had at 41⅜. However, as the Windsor broker walked away from the post, Larry quoted the market 41½–⅞. Actually there were no orders on his book to buy stock at 41½. The 41½ bid was a nominal one inserted for his own account for the sake of providing continuity and depth into the market.

A broker who had been observing the proceedings and waiting to place an order now stepped into the crowd. Suspecting the new bid to be the specialist's, he speaks. "I have a bid for 1,000 ZAP at 41½."

"Right. The market's 41½–⅞. It's your bid." So saying Larry withdrew his own bid because whenever he has a valid public bid on his books at a given price he is not permitted to bid for his own account at that price.

Thus it went for well over an hour. In the process the stock sold as low as 39⅜ before some spirited bidding moved the stock back to 41. When the bulk of the crowd finally dissipated, Larry looked in our direction and smiled.

"How did you like the show? Sorry I couldn't talk to you sooner but a writer for the *Wall Street Recorder* really zapped ZAP this morning. He inferred they were using questionable accounting practices to inflate earnings. Personally, I don't think he is right, but in any event, it certainly stirred up excitement.

"It's a good thing, I suppose, in that it might cause some real accountants to analyze ZAP's books. It's a great little company. Maybe all this excitement will encourage some good buying in the stock after this initial selling pressure subsides."

Looking at us he asks, "Would you like to know how we operate? Fine, I don't know how much you were able to pick up while watching so we'll just start at the beginning. First of all, I am a member of the American Stock Exchange. That means that I do not work for the Exchange. Instead I'm in business for myself.

"The Exchange supervises me. They tell me how to run my business. They tell me what I can and cannot do, and how to go about it. But the money it takes to operate this business is my money and the profits or losses that accrue are my profits or losses, not the Exchange's.

"Although I'm in business for myself strictly speaking I don't work alone. Instead I have five partners. Together we are called a 'specialist unit.' Here is Mike Getz and Vic Cibala on my left. On my right, I'd like you to meet Sammy Berger, Gene Anthony and Will Leifer. Working together as a unit we are assigned a total of 51 stocks, of which ZAP is just one.

"Will Leifer and I are the senior partners in the unit. I personally handle ZAP and 7 other stocks while my partners handle the others.

"That term 'book' is probably misleading to you because we use the term interchangably to mean at least three different things. First of all, when I refer to our 'book' what I mean is the 51 stocks the Exchange has assigned our unit to handle.

"We also use the term in reference to the open orders brokers leave with us for future execution. For instance, if you give your broker an order to buy 100 shares of stock at 19½ when the stock is selling at 20, obviously your order will not be executed because a person would be a fool to sell his stock to you for 19½ if someone else is willing to pay him $20. Therefore, your broker will leave the order with us. Then, if and when the stock sells down to 19½, we are responsible to your broker for buying your stock just as soon as any orders ahead of yours at 19½ have been filled.

"See these cubbyholes under the counter of my post? The pieces of paper in them are order tickets brokers have left with me. While you were watching all the activity in ZAP a little while ago, you probably saw me thumbing through these tickets from time to time marking them, adding to them or taking them out as the orders they represented were either executed or canceled.

"The third 'book' we refer to is the only real book we have in a physical sense. That is the little spiral bound notebook you see here in front of me. This is the book into which we enter details of all the stock we buy and sell for our own account. We keep one of these books for each of our 51 stocks using it as a journal of original entry for all our personal transactions.

"ZAP has what we call a good book. Invariably there are numerous orders both to buy or to sell at all prices close to the market. For instance, the stock just traded at 41 and the quote is now 40⅞–41. I've got orders to buy ZAP in depth all the way down to 35. Look at this. Three tickets to buy at 40⅞, five at 40¾, others at 40⅝, ½, ¼, ⅛, 40, 39¾, ⅝, ⅜, and so forth.

"The same thing holds true on the sell side. Of course, the book to sell right now is heavier than usual because of this morning's article but no matter which way the market goes, the book is heavy. This helps me to make a good close market in the stock.

"ZAP is also what we specialists call a 'ticket writer' because usually all we have to do is match the orders on our book against market orders as they come in. We don't have to take big positions in stocks like this, so our risk and exposure is usually much less than it is with less active stocks.

"The kind of stock we specialists prefer not to have is a stock like Drag products here. Drag is really a drag for us. It last traded the day before yesterday at 24⅝. Right now I'm quoting it 24⅜–⅞, my bid and offer. On the buy side, the best bid I have is for 100 shares at 24⅛. There is another 400 at 23⅞, then nothing down to 23¼ where there are 300 shares. On the sell side the book is just as thin. The best offer I've got is 500 to sell at 25½.

"This is the kind of stock that makes nobody happy. The public doesn't like it because it is too volatile. They are afraid to trade it because the price jumps around a lot. Unfortunately they think I am playing games with them and it's easy to see why they feel that way.

"The company is disappointed because they think the price drops too quickly whenever anyone sells. Of course, it goes up just as fast on buying, but no one ever complains about rising prices. All these complaints eventually get back to me in one form or another.

"I don't like these wide swings or the low volume either but I have no way of making this stock look or trade like AT&T. Because there is such a thin book, I've got to trade the stock for my own account more than I desire. In fact, I often have bigger positions in Drag than

I do in ZAP even though ZAP is at least a dozen times more active.

"The kind of stock I like to have, the ideal one, of course, is one where I never have to buy or sell even one share for my own account unless I want to. But this is an impossible dream. I'm well-satisfied if a stock trades at least 2,000 shares a day, with at least 30 per cent to 45 per cent of all orders entered being limit orders.

"Now look at my personal trading book. On the left side I list all the stock I've bought while details of my selling are entered on the right side. Up here, at the top of the page is my opening position. In this particular stock, I started the day long 783 shares. So far today, I've bought 500 shares in round lots, 100 at 14⅞, 200 at 14¾ and 200 at 14⅝; also 73 shares in odd lots. On the sell side I've sold only 100 shares at 14¾ and 46 shares in odd lots so that as of now I'm long 1,210 shares.

"In addition to noting the time and price of each trade I make, I've got to note the name of the broker with whom I traded and whether or not I stabilized the market with my trade. At the end of each day I have to make a photocopy of this book and give it to the trading analysts on the Exchange staff. They review all our trades to see that we don't break any rules. In this respect and many others, the staff here runs a very tight ship. Much tighter than most people suspect.

"Actually this close daily supervision works to our benefit because it not only keeps all of us honest, but it keeps us from getting sloppy. When we get sloppy not only does the public not get the kind of market it deserves but we don't do as well financially.

"Insofar as what I'm supposed to be doing, I've got a number of very important functions and responsibilities. First of all, my partners and I are required to make fair and orderly markets in our 51 stocks. This means that when you come in to buy or sell one of my stocks 'at the market' you can be sure of getting the best price available anywhere in the world at the instant your order is executed. That price might be better or worse than it was 5 minutes earlier, or than it will be 30 seconds from now, but now, for this instant, it is the best price you can get anywhere.

"For instance, if you wanted to buy 100 shares of a stock that just traded at 20 and the best order to sell on my book is now 20½, I'm not supposed to allow you to pay 20½ because that would cause the stock to move ½ point on just 100 shares. The Exchange considers a move of this size to be excessive for a $20 stock. Therefore it requires me to sell stock out of my inventory to you at perhaps 20⅛ or 20¼.

I've got to do this whether I want to or not and whether or not I have the stock in my inventory. If I have no stock in my inventory, then I am expected to go 'short' rather than permit you to pay 20½. If I refuse to do this, I am going to get called down for it. If that happens too often and I can't justify what I've done, I can expect the Exchange to discipline me in some way.

"The term for this is called stabilizing the market. We are not permitted to buy or sell stock for our own accounts indiscriminately. Instead, a specialist is supposed to buy or sell stock for his own account only when it is reasonably necessary to do so.

"We stabilize the market, for instance, by selling you stock at 20¼ instead of allowing you to pay 20½ from the lowest seller on our book, and by buying stock when you come in to sell thereby giving you a higher price closer to the last sale when the best public bidder on our book may be bidding a much lower price. All this is done in such a way as to modify as much as possible any changes in price from one trade to the next.

"As a result of the buying and selling we do, the average price change between trades is only about 9 cents. This is much better than it was back in the early sixties. In those days, specialists had much more flexibility of action. Unfortunately, this flexibility was abused so that now we have to work under rules that are often quite onerous.

"Stabilizing the market also means that a specialist should not sell stock from his inventory at a price lower than the last selling price, or buy stock for his own account at a higher selling price except under unusual and strictly defined conditions. The reason for this prohibition is to prevent a specialist from changing the direction of a market trend on his own volition.

"The only time a trade in a stock should take place is when someone other than myself initiates it. This is done whenever a broker comes in with a market order either to buy or sell one of my stocks or with a limit order at a price that enables me to offset it against an open order already on my book. For example, when you were watching the ZAP crowd in action, you should have noticed that some of the brokers were waiting to buy while others were waiting to sell. If you were really observant you would also have noted that, although I knew who the buyers and sellers were and probably could guess approximately the quantity of stock they wanted to trade, I never made a move to initiate a trade. The first move always had to come from one of those brokers. All I could do was respond to their overtures once they were made by accepting their orders. Then I either matched them against orders on my book or took the stock in to my personal account.

"All these restrictions and prohibitions make it tough for any specialist to manipulate the market for his own advantage the way so many people seem to think we do. We aren't allowed to bid prices up or to knock them down any more like the old timers did. We are so restricted that we are in effect nothing more than residual buyers and sellers of stock whenever the supply/demand equation gets out of balance. This is the way that we moderate price swings and make the market more orderly.

"In essence we act as auctioneers continually attempting to adjust prices up and down in response to both buying and selling pressures in an orderly, rational manner so that as many transactions as possible can be made at prices that are mutually satisfactory to both the buyer and the seller.

"Whenever buying or selling causes a stock to move from one general price range to the next, we try to see that the move is accomplished in an orderly manner with price changes between individual trades as narrow as possible.

"The only thing I have to work with is the capital at my disposal and the orders on my book. The 'fair market value' of any of my stocks, so far as I am concerned is within the range of the highest public bid and lowest public offer on my book at any particular time. This is the fair market because this is the price at which people actually are willing to exchange stock for money at this instant. Therefore, this is the only relevant price. As a specialist I don't care about book values, work out values, price-earnings ratios or anything else. I can't afford to concern myself with any of these things that theoretically are supposed to affect what people ought to be doing. But I do have to very sensitive to what they actually are doing or I'll soon be broke.

"A lot of people seem to think that there is a conflict of interest in our business merely because we both execute open orders on behalf of the public and trade for our own account. However, when they come to understand the real and constricting restrictions under which we must operate, they realize this potential for conflict is more apparent than real.

"If I am prohibited at times from trading when I would like to, then, if I am forced to trade because the market demands this of me when I don't want to, on balance there is very little harm I can do. If I cannot step ahead of orders on my book to trade for my account, I cannot affect the trend of the market. If everything I do is done to modify or inhibit what otherwise would be more volatile moves in stocks, and if my activities are closely supervised, which I believe they are, than my activities can serve only to be regarded as beneficial."

Profile of a Specialist

To be successful a specialist requires a number of attributes most normal people neither have nor seem capable of developing.

First of all a good specialist must invariably have a nervous system attuned to the short-term resolution of business decisions involving huge sums of money. Next, to be brutally frank, he must personally possess or have access to more money than brains. Few normal human beings would willingly expose the large sums of money required in this business at the high risk and for the meager returns that poor market years bring on.

At the same time, very few men of economic means would voluntarily permit people with little experience at handling large sums of money, who have never tasted the bitterness of large monetary losses, to set up for them, the parameters under which to do business. Yet this is what specialists in recent years have permitted to occur. The serious indiscretions of a few specialists in the past have signalled to the honest and progressive specialist the need for closer supervision of the market. For many years specialists appeared to operate with little or no supervision. Now, the pendulum has swung in the other direction. Today specialists can only operate in a tightly controlled, clearly defined manner, often leaving them very little to say about the deployment of their funds. Because of their clear-cut obligation to the market they often know in advance that a position they are about to take will result in a loss. Nevertheless, they have no choice but to act this way in the public interest or to look for a new line of work.

To compound their difficulties, specialists never have been effective spokesmen. Certainly they have had no one to speak on their behalf as effectively as dozens of their detractors. Over the years, people have attacked them for all sorts of reasons. Writers in search of an exciting story and politicians in search of an issue to catapult them into office as well as numerous others have found the specialist to be fair game.

In all fairness, however, the blame should not always be placed on the shoulders of the detractors because when a specialist is given an occasional opportunity to present his story he has seldom risen to the challenge. For whatever reason he often presents his case in such a way that makes his detractors appear at least partially correct in their assessment of him.

Let's consider a specific case. Some time ago a stock dropped 27 points at the opening. After closing at 162 on the previous Friday, it opened at 135 on 20,500 shares. On the surface, without knowing any of the circumstances surrounding the transaction, this appears to be an abominably poor execution. This, in fact, may or may not be true. We don't know because the facts on which to make a judgment have not been made public. It also appears to be a situation where the specialist failed to do his job because the drop occurred not as the result of any adverse announcement by the company but on an announcement of higher earnings. However, the higher earnings figures were not up to the level some people had anticipated. This caused some large institutional investors irrationally and impetuously to dump the stock.

The reporter who chronicled this event is considered fair and responsible. He contacted the specialist for some insights as to what happened. Being a good reporter, he asked a question he knew they were forbidden to answer, but which, nevertheless, had a bearing on the story. He wanted to know the size of the specialist's position. Rather than diplomatically backing away, the specialist's comment reportedly was only that it was "big enough."

Pressing, the reporter said that many people thought he had

abandoned the stock by not buying it in sufficient quantities all the way down. To this the specialist caustically replied: "That's for them to say and me to know. I don't think the public has any right to know what the situation is. We performed—we must have—because there was no comment from the Stock Exchange."

A remark of this nature is not out of place on the Exchange Floor. Down there everyone is direct and to the point. Business is transacted so quickly that there is no time for the subtleties that abound in other areas. But however proper in substance the specialist's answer might have been, a more circuitous reply was in order. If the specialist had any public relations sensitivity whatever, he would have said that there is a strategic danger in publicly announcing his position. Consequently, not only he but Exchange officials as well are prohibited from giving such information. For instance, if the specialist did indeed have a large position which was revealed to the public, a smart professional might be able to determine how much excess liquidity the specialist was likely to have. Then he could use this knowledge to manipulate the price of this or some other stock in the specialist's unit. The other side of the coin, of course, is that if the specialist's performance was poor, withholding the necessary information will prevent outsiders from ever finding out about it.

A more responsible, far less cavalier attitude to the press was noted on another occasion when this same reporter chronicled the story of another stock which also went through the purgatory of massive selling. Here is his story:

One day, just before noon, over 10,000 shares of stock were offered for sale. The specialist was surprised because this particular stock normally trades only about 700 to 800 shares per day. Obviously, the offer to sell was extraordinary and, under the rules, the specialist contacted the nearest floor governor. Trading was halted and, a representative from the Amex Securities Division called the company to see if they could explain the reason for the sudden pressure on the stock. There was a reason. Third quarter earnings were going to be down significantly.

The company, at the request of the Exchange issued an announcement but coyly failed to say by how much earnings would be down. Dissatisfied with this, the Exchange refused to permit the stock to reopen. Finally, after the close, the company announced third quarter earnings would be about $140,000 or 13 cents per share compared to

$358,00 or 29 cents the previous year. Additionally, company officials implied the fourth quarter would be just as bad.

Within minutes after the block hit the Floor, the Exchange had its answer. It halted trading pending the announcement. Significantly no other stock came in to sell up to this point suggesting to the reporter that if someone did get the word early, he attemped to act before the word spread. Unfortunately for the seller, the Exchange acted even faster.

Prior to the trading halt the stock closed at 22½. Obviously, because of the light trading, a 10,000 share sell order was going to have a tremendous impact on the price.

Fortunately, the specialist who explained what happened was one of those who has a facility with words as well as numbers. He pointed out that because of the low level of trading as well as the small number of shares outstanding, a 10,000 share order to sell is equivalent to a block of several hundred thousand shares in many Big Board stocks with broader public distribution.

He pointed out that the specialist handling this stock either bought or sold stock in 75 per cent of all transactions. This is significantly above the Exchange average and means that he is subject to much greater financial risk.

The adverse announcement triggered other selling until on the afternoon of the second day there were approximately 125,000 shares for sale between $10 and $15. Fortunately, there was offsetting buying interest. Enough, in fact, at $13 to permit the specialist to reopen the stock on a block of 92,000 shares of which he purchased over 10,000 shares. It was reported that the stock traded actively after the reopening in a range between 12½ and 14 and that the specialist, though he sold out the stock he purchased at the opening lost money because of the inventory he had prior to the halt.

This last statement was mildly challenged by the reporter but it is entirely logical. For instance, let us assume that the specialist had only 1,000 shares in inventory prior to the halt. If he paid just 22½ for the stock, he had a paper loss of $9,500 when the stock reopened at 13. Then, if he was able to sell all 10,000 shares he purchased at the reopening at 13¾, which would be an extremely high average price, he would have made only $7,500 to offset his $9,500 loss. Thus he still had a $2,000 loss for all his efforts.

Why, when he already had an inventory did he buy more at the opening? Said the specialist: "He must anticipate his post-opening demands and buy enough stock to meet these demands in the after market. It's a guess, and, believe me, it's a risk."

Here was a literate, reasoned answer to a legitimate question of why something that seemed very unreasonable had occurred. The reporter was given access to much more data than normally is made public but in this particular instance the release of confidential data was well-served. Not to have made it available might again have left an erroneous impression in the mind of the public.

Because of danger of misuse, the specialist position statistics are treated as highly confidential by the Amex. No one is permitted access to this data except the specialist himself, his clerical employees, a few staff members whose jobs require them to have such information, and authorized S.E.C. staffers when specifically requested for official S.E.C. purposes.

Requests from company officials for this information are shelved as diplomatically as possible until sufficient time has elapsed for the information to have no tactical benefit should someone attempt to use it to influence the price of the stock. Of course, the Exchange recognizes that most such requests are the result of legitimate company concern. Nevertheless, because such information might be misused, it is necessary to handle it with the utmost caution.

Because of this very real need to be discreet, it was entirely proper for the first specialist to refrain from directly answering some of the reporter's most penetrating questions. But the sort of answers he gave didn't do him or the Exchange he represented any good in the eyes of the newspaper's readers. The responses he made could serve only to reinforce the public's ideas of a "public be damned" attitude.

An example of the risks specialists as a group are sometimes called upon to make occurred during the depth of the bear market in May, 1970. At that time, with the market crashing, with the smell of panic in the air, all specialist units were up to their ears in stock that no one else wanted. Inventory positions of $3 million to $5 million per unit were common. Some units had positions several times that amount.

This was a time when several Wall Street brokerage firms had already collapsed. Others were either on the verge of failing or rumored to be so. One of Wall Street's stellar brokerage houses, Goodbody & Company had been absorbed by Merrill Lynch.

Dozens of other lesser known firms either had folded or had been merged out of existence. Outside of Wall Street, the Penn Central went into bankruptcy. Lockheed was saved at the very brink of failure by an extraordinary government insured loan. Rumors were rampant that Pan Am World Airways and Trans World Airlines also were about to sink. Interest rates were at the highest levels in one hundred years with the the supply of money to all but the highest rated firms not only prohibitively expensive but almost impossible to obtain.

Had one cared to bet on it, he would have found more and more people willing to wager that some day soon total disaster would occur on a day so gloomy that not even the sun would rise again.

Under the circumstances, anyone with a normal mentality undoubtedly would have copped out of the market long ago. He would have sold out his inventory positions for whatever they would bring; would have paid off his borrowers if any; and if he had $5 million, put it into tax-free municipal bonds. Since many such tax-free bonds were yielding 7 per cent or more at that time, he would have been assured a tax-free $350,000 after tax return without the risk and the aggravation that came with trying to make orderly markets when no basis for orderly markets existed. Of the 35 specialist units, there was not one which achieved an income of this proportion in 1970. The majority lost money.

Instead of copping out, specialists not only threw their own money in to support the market but they borrowed to the hilt in a desperate effort to keep the dam from bursting. At the peak of this panic, the junior members of some units had not only lost their investment in the unit but had paper losses in the tens or hundreds of thousands of dollars.

Had they or their creditors heeded the voices of doom and closed up their shop at this point, it would have taken these men the rest of their lives to pay off their creditors. As it was, except for a few ulcers, everyone stuck it out because there was really nothing else they could do. In the explosive rally that occurred in the second half of 1970, many specialists not only worked off their losses but turned in profits nearly handsome enough to make all their anguish worthwhile. They proved again that the ultimate secret of Wall Street success is staying power.

Critics of the specialist system conveniently choose to overlook the real and enormous risks that regularly appear. They choose instead to focus on isolated short-term profits, which when viewed out of context, sometimes do seem inordinately large. Conveniently, the critics fail to offset these profits against the losses that are a regular part of this business.

Another favorite tactic is to pick out an individual transaction which when taken out of context appears to make a good cause for the bankruptcy of the system. But while on the surface, any one particular trade might not seem good, it is difficult either to defend or condemn it without knowing all the details surrounding the particular trade.

Then, too, trades that often seem entirely logical when made under the pressures of the moment can sometimes look rather silly when viewed in the cold, clear, aftersight of the future. But this is not a trait of just the securities business.

It appears to me that the thing to keep in mind is that there is a world of difference between an occasional case of poor judgment and a deliberate intent to defraud. When criticizing or suggesting changes in a system that has proved its value over the centuries, great care should be employed to distinguish between the two.

Criticism of the system also arises because of honest differences of opinion as to what constitutes adequate depth in the market. Sometimes even specialists in a single unit may differ here.

Still other persons criticize specialists for permitting the market to do what it was designed to do, namely to move both up and down. Some of the most vocal arguments against specialists in recent years have come from people who have made their job difficult by deliberately bidding stocks up needlessly high then complaining bitterly when their equally intensive selling causes these same stocks to fall just as dramatically. These critics apparently want to believe the job of the specialist is to allow stocks to move up, then support them there. To them, a decline in price is unthinkable, at least, until they sell out their own positions.

Although intellectualism sometimes does seem to be missing, specialists possess something much more necessary to their success and survival. The man who makes it as a specialist possesses an instinct for trading which few other people have.

A good specialist knows, almost to the second, how long to give a stock a tight, orderly market. He can sense exactly when to step aside in the face of an overwhelming trend that will carry a stock to its next level of support or demand. Were he to attempt to run his business with an instinct less well-developed it could be quite costly as the average investor learns to his regret time and time again.

A good specialist can recall trading sequences that have occurred months, sometimes years back. A good specialist judges the competence of buyers and sellers he has never met by the brokers they choose, the way they instruct their brokers to enter orders, and the manner in which they choose to buy and sell.

He knows at all times his inventory position in each stock. He knows the average cost of his inventory and has an uncanny ability to revalue his average cost after every trade he makes. He can remember the size of his open orders, not only at the market but at virtually every level above and below the market.

A good specialist has a corrosion-proof stomach. He has to because the tensions he faces would fell a lesser man.

He has to believe that so long as he stays tuned in to what the market is saying to him, he will eventually show a profit. He never can allow himself the pleasure of becoming despondent about his interim losses even though they might amount to tens or hundreds of thousands of dollars at times.

Larry sometimes tells the story of one of his wife's relatives. This man is reputed to have both made and lost over a million dollars three or four times during his long career as specialist. To become wealthy, this man counseled, a man had to have a contempt for money. He thought that too many people developed such an overriding fear of losing the little they had, that it inhibited their ability both to recover existing losses and to go on to make really big profits when the opportunity presented itself.

As a specialist, Larry is a member of the American Stock Exchange. He is one of six partners in what is known as a specialist unit. All six partners are Amex members. A specialist unit though called a partnership is more correctly a joint venture arrangement where each participant of the unit shares in the profits or losses of that unit according to a predetermined formula. In total there are approximately 165 specialists banded together in approximately 35 specialist units of which Larry's unit is typical.

In Larry's unit, he and his partner, Wilbur Leifer are the senior partners. Both have a 37.5 per cent stake in the profits or losses of the unit. A third partner, Gene Anthony has a 10 per cent interest while the remaining three partners, Sammy Berger, Vic Cibola and Michael

Getz are 5 per cent partners. The latter three, however, are not real partners in the true sense of the word because of the unique arrangement they have with the joint venture which makes them more like employees who have a profit sharing arrangement. The arrangement is such that during poor years, for as long as they are permitted to remain with the unit, they will receive a minimum annual draw of $20,000 each. On the other hand, whenever the profit of the unit exceeds $400,000, they are entitled to 5 per cent of the earnings which of course will raise their earnings above the $20,000 level.

About 1965 the Exchange began an aggressive effort to strengthen the financial capabilities of all specialist units. In line with this effort, it began a campaign to persuade and pressure smaller one and two man units to consolidate with other units.

The net result of these efforts was to have the same number of specialists with the same amount of capital. But these aggregates of capital were consolidated into fewer but larger ventures. They discerned that larger units would enable the specialist system to withstand more effectively the pressures caused by the greater institutionalization of the market, and that it would give the specialists the kind of safety and flexibility that can be achieved only through diversification. This would permit specialists to utilize more effectvely their resources while at the same time permit them to maintain better quality markets in the face of increasing volume.

As a result of these pressures Larry's father-in-law decided to merge with an old friend, Saul Leifer and his son Wilbur. Will was the third generation Leifer in the business. Both units had about the same number of stocks and both were equally manned.

In 1967 the growth of over-all Exchange volume and the surge of new listings began to put pressures on the unit. Although both families had sufficient capital in reserve to handle whatever needs the market placed on them, they were not physically able to handle much more than the load they were then carrying. Unless they picked up a new partner, it was quite likely the Exchange would not continue giving the unit its share of new listings as they became available.

Consequently, the unit decided to look for a new partner. Their search ended when Larry received a call from his college roommate Gene Anthony. Gene had gone into pro football after college but he was looking to find a permanent career.

Unlike many athletes, Gene had been a serious, better than average student in college. He was a math major who, as anyone who ever watched him or played against him could testify, was equally quick on his feet as he was with his numbers. The partners thought that if he could prove to be as quick with the auction process as he was on the gridiron he would make a good partner provided he was interested.

Interested he was. The few times he went on the Floor, the Exchange seemed even more exciting to him than a pro football game. Therefore, it was no surprise when he accepted the offer to join the unit almost without hesitation.

Next, Will brought in Michael Getz, a hot shot security analyst friend. Mike has a Ph.D., so he became perhaps the best educated specialist on the Floor. On his way to the Ph.D. he had majored both in psychology and investments, giving him an unbeatable educational combination for this business.

Because he did not have money of his own to purchase a membership, the money to buy his seat was advanced under a subordinated loan agreement with Will's father. Under this agreement, Mike was advanced the money needed to purchase his seat. He was obligated by the agreement first to pay off the cost of his seat, and, then, to contribute a predetermined amount of capital to the unit.

Soon after this both senior men decided to retire. Both offered to give their seats to the clerks who had worked for them over the years. Since neither Sammy Berger nor Victor Cibola had any money to contribute, they were brought in on the basis of the expertise they had demonstrated in working for the unit over the years. They were offered a 5 per cent share of earnings with a guaranteed minimum draw of $20,000.

Their seats, however, were transferred to them under what is known as an ABC agreement which contains no provision for a greater future share of profits or for a positive requirement that they purchase their seats.

Under the ABC arrangement the latter two partners have three options with respect to their seats.

First of all, if either should ever decide to leave the unit for any reason and wants to keep his seat, he may either reimburse the unit with enough money to purchase another seat at the time or he would himself have to purchase a seat in the open market to give to the unit.

Second, if either one decided to leave the Exchange altogether, he could sell his seat and turn the proceeds over to the unit, or—

Third, as in the case of the senior partners who turned the seats over to them, the seat could be transferred to someone else who would become affiliated with the unit. In this event Sammy and Vic would be paid a nominal amount for having to relinquish their seats.

As to age, the unit is one of the younger units. All the partners are in their thirties except Sammy who is 41. Sammy is also the senior member of the unit when it comes to Exchange longevity, with 25 years of Floor experience behind him. He had worked for Wilbur's father continuously since he was 16 years old.

At the time of the Exchange reorganization in 1962, the average specialist was about 58 years old. Competent but too calcified in their ways to adapt to the pressures and demands of the 1960s, many specialists decided to retire early in order to trade in board rooms rather than play a game which appeared to be too heavily weighed against them.

The unit's educational spectrum is broader than average, ranging from the doctorate of Getz to the eleventh grade education of Sammy. In between, Larry at 37 holds a bachelor's degree in sociology and Gene holds one in mathematics. Wilbur was an Air Force captain and an aeronautical engineer. He graduated from the Air Force Academy while Vic has been attending evening sessions for years at N.Y.U. trying to complete the requirements for his degree.

From what has just been said, it should be apparent that the principal market making element is not the specialist but the specialist unit. In recent years the number of such units has stabilized at about 35, down from about 50 in 1962. Each of these units consists of at least 3 specialists. The average unit has 5 specialists while the two or three largest units might have as many as 10 or more partners at times.

Stocks are assigned by the Exchange not to a specialist but to a specialist unit. Thus, any stock the unit gets is assigned to the Harkins-Leifer unit even though within the unit Gene, Vic or one of the other partners might in fact be the specialist in charge.

The specialists affiliate into units for a number of reasons other than just the pressures exerted by the Exchange.

First and foremost to the specialists, there are economic reasons for merging. It has been demonstrated statistically that with adequately capitalized units of three to six men, the risk to the unit is minimized. Units of this size face the probability of losing money on balance no more than one or two quarters each three to five years. With only one or two partners, this risk is much greater. On the other hand whenever the units get too big, they may become too unwieldly and personality conflicts are more likely to develep. This may reduce the unit's efficiency.

Next, capital requirements in the business are not only highly variable but conditions regularly come up where it takes more money to make a good market in a stock than most individuals can get their hands on. Therefore, affiliations of specialists into units allows greater pools of capital to be assembled to maintain more orderly markets when individual stocks are under great strain and pressure. Sometimes the pressures can become so great that even these greater pools of capital become overburdened as the markets of 1969–1970 demonstrated.

The amalgamation of specialists into units allows for greater diversification and diffusion of specialist risk, because with a greater number of stocks to work with a loss in one stock will create a smaller drain on a unit's over-all capital than would be true of any single specialist's capital position. At the same time, the probabilities are increased that some other stocks in the unit are sufficiently profitable to offset the effects of the loss.

This has importance not only to the specialist but to investors as well. Under the current regulatory attitude, specialists are forced to maintain markets on behalf of the public in such a manner that they often know when initiating a trade that the trade will be contrary to their own best interests. They know from the start they will lose money on many transactions.

Therefore, the inventory of stocks assigned to a unit has to be sufficiently broad to provide it at all times with at least a few stocks that are likely to be sufficiently profitable to offset the losses resulting from other more difficult to manage stocks.

Finally units make it easier to match the personality and trading characteristics of a stock with the personality, expertise and temperament of a specialist. Just as personalities of individuals vary, so do the characteristics of stocks vary from one stock to the next. Some are actively traded, some are not. Some stocks are volatile while others rarely if ever change a great deal in price regardless of their volume of trading or the state of the market.

At times stocks become aggressive, hostile, flamboyant and unruly. If one specialist in a unit finds he suddenly has difficulty handling a stock he can turn it over to one of his partners. As an individual specialist, however, he could not afford to ask the Exchange to reallocate the stock to someone else because this would be considered a public admission of his incompetence.

To become a specialist, a man first has to become a member of the Exchange. This means he either must find an existing member who is willing to sell his seat; he has to find someone to buy his seat for him in the open market; or he has to find someone to turn over an existing seat to him. Prior to taking title to his seat, the prospective member must submit to a rather extensive characer investigation by the Exchange and only when he successfully passes this, is his name brought to a vote by the membership.

For a specialist candidate, however, it is rather pointless to become an Exchange member unless he has prior assurance from an existing specialist unit that he will be accepted as a partner in the unit. Becoming a specialist involves spending some time down on the Floor working as a clerk, usually for the unit where the candidate ultimately will become affiliated.

Under close scrutiny, when the partners are convinced the man is ready to be taken into the unit, they will sponsor him for membership and arrange to have him take the specialist qualifying exam. When he passes the tests, they sign the necessary papers admitting him into the unit.

Many of the men who are specialists today are individuals who over the years have accumulated sufficient money to bankroll their share of the unit's capital. This is virtually an impossibility for newcomers today.

Many specialists today are bankrolled by member firms which are looking to diversify. They view specializing as a potential new "profit center." Such firms may buy a membership for one of their more successful over-the-counter traders whom they then install on the Floor; they might sign on a competent Floor Trader; or they might acquire an active specialist unit and make its members partners or stockholders in the member firm.

For many years specialists either were "loners" or members of specialist firms that consisted of specialists active on both exchanges. It is only in recent years that member firms which do a public business, underwrite stock and bond issues, manage mutual funds and perform other related brokerage functions have also become a factor in specializing.

Until recently such public houses have not involved themselves in this area.

As volume increased during the 1960s, the greater financial demands placed on specialists found more and more units with a need for mass infusions of new capital. Many excellent specialists just did not have the kind of money the new markets demanded. Of those who did possess the necessary capital, fewer were willing to risk their entire fortunes in a business that was becoming ever more restrictive on their activities even when they were doing nothing that could be considered improper.

Since specialists are not employed by the Exchanges, any losses they accrue are their own. They cannot afford to be public spirited citizens willing to support the investment of the investing public regardless of personal cost. Therefore, some means had to be found to generate the capital needed to conduct this business on a sound basis. It costs much more to get into this business today than it did even 10 years ago. Furthermore, at times the risks are astronomical, but then in good years, so are the profits. Recognizing this, while at the same time looking for new profit centers, more and more "public houses" began to consider specializing.

When this became a practical necessity, it was discovered that a firm doing a public brokerage business could resolve the dilemma of possible conflict of interest by refraining from recommending, soliciting or otherwise having anything to do in a sales capacity with those few companies in which they have a specialist interest. If a brokerage firm entering a specialist unit found it was an underwriter or financial advisor to one of the companies in the unit, the firm was given its choice of giving up their underwriting relationship or having the stock assgned to another unit.

The Manufacturing of Stock

BEFORE GOING any farther, it will be well at this point to gain some insights as to how stocks that sometimes are so casually traded come into existence. It is important to remember that not even one share of stock in any company can be bought or sold until that share first formally comes into existence. Each share of stock has to be manufactured or created through a complicated legal process. Once created, the share of stock continues to exist forever or until some other legal act occurs to cause its demise.

This is not just self-evident but basic to an understanding of how the market functions and why prices of stocks are continually changing. Although it is so basic and obvious, like so many other fundamentals, it often seems to be overlooked by many people. Unlike a deposit in a savings account, a share of stock does not just come into being from some inexhaustible spring at the time an investor makes a purchase only to disappear conveniently into thin air when he decides to sell.

At a savings bank, the level of deposits is variable. It is what economists call "elastic." The level of deposits depends on the acts of individuals who continuously are making deposits of money into and withdrawals of money out of their accounts. The over-all level of deposits at a bank increases as additions are made to savings accounts while the growth of deposits is inhibited and declines by the amount of withdrawals. Because of this interchange, the level of deposits is fluid and ever changing.

Because the level of deposits is fluid, pressures on the banking system can easily be adjusted by printing or withdrawing money from circulation. This causes the value of deposits as measured in dollars to be stable. As a result, the number of dollars you put into a bank account will be the number you will eventually withdraw. This amount will be modified only by the amount of interest, if any, paid by the bank on the account.

When it comes to stocks on the other hand, the supply of stock in a particular company is, for all practical purposes, fixed rather than variable. The number of shares outstanding can change but this is a complicated process which occurs only at rare intervals rather than continuously. With stocks then, what changes, and what causes the big swings in the prices of stocks is a variation in the level of demand for a particular stock.

There are times when it seems as though virtually everyone in the world wants to buy a given stock at one and the same time. Because the supply of stock available is limited to that owned by present shareholders, those who want to buy stock must bid enough to induce some owner to sell. This drives the price to a point high enough to release the precise amount of stock sought by the most eager and aggressive bidder.

At other times when everyone seems to want to sell, while only a continuously diminishing number of investors care to buy, the price drops lower, then lower until it reaches a level where some bargain hunter will condescend to trade his money for the shares being offered by the most desperate seller.

As we have said, each share of stock in existence today was created just once. It will continue to exist as a single share until something happens to cause a fundamental change. The stock might be split in which case it will become more than one share. The company might declare a "reverse split" in which case it will become less than one share. Other alternatives may cause the shares to disappear altogether.

Once created and issued to a "shareholder," that is anyone who is legally entitled to own the stock, the share of stock will always remain the property of someone just as a home once constructed is always owned by someone until it is destroyed.

Whenever a shareholder wants to sell his stock, he cannot, except in rare cases, return it to the company for a refund of his purchase price in the way he closes out his bank account in return for a check for the amount of his deposit. Instead, once he buys a stock, a stockholder can only dispose of it by giving or selling it to someone else. Therefore, to provide some sort of mechanism to allow for the transfer of stock ownership from an existing shareholder to a new one, some means for effecting this change quickly and efficiently had to be created. The mechanism created to meet this need is called the stock transfer process and it may take place either on a stock exchange or "over-the-counter."

Each company that has "gone public," that is each company which is partially or wholly owned by shareholders other than the people who founded it, makes use of the "public markets" to transfer ownership from owner to owner.

Most securities generally trade in "round lots" or standard trading units of 100 shares. Investors wishing to trade in lesser units do so in odd lots on which a slight premium is charged.

Each of the more than 3,000 companies listed on the two national stock exchanges have at least one class of securities which have been listed in a formal manner. That one issue usually is the common stock.

The value of any stock is further complicated because each company individually determines for itself the total number of shares it will issue. The company in cooperation with its underwriter also has much to say about the initial selling price. There is absolutely no uniformity here. Every company may have a different number of shares outstanding. This has an important bearing on the price because as we have seen when a stock becomes popular, its price has a tendency to rise. This tendency becomes especially pronounced if a small number of shares are available. Because of the difference in the number of shares available for sale, the stock of two equally popular stocks might rise in price at different rates. The stock with fewer shares available for sale would probably increase in value faster than the other issue.

Stocks trade on an Exchange through a formal process known as "listing." The prerequisite listing requirements center around whether or not a company is of sufficient financial stature with its stock sufficiently distributed among a large number of shareholders to benefit from a regulated, public auction market.

First of all, a company has to have demonstrated the ability to make money under competitive conditions. The Amex expects that its companies will be able to report net earnings of at least $400,000 per year with net tangible assets totaling at least $4 million.

The company also has to have sufficient "public" distribution. In other words, in addition to whatever amount of stock is held by officers and founders of the company, there has to be at least 400,000 shares of stock worth at least $3 million on the open market and distributed among at least 1,200 shareholders. These minimum public distribution figures are very important as the basis for judging depth in the market. Without adequate depth, the market will not function as well as the public expects nor will the specialist perform as efficiently as he both wants and is expected to.

Whenever a company belives it meets these initial requirements plus a number of other qualitative standards, it may apply for listing.

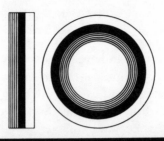

Stocks—The Lifeblood of the Specialist

T HE CONTINUED profitability of a specialist unit, its lifeblood if you will, lies in the number of actively traded stocks assigned to the unit. It is not a generally recognized fact but the list of stocks trading on the Amex is much more volatile than the raw statistical figures would indicate. Because of the constant flux in the composition of the stock list, every unit is continuously losing stocks that potentially represent an important profit base to the unit.

To get an idea of the dynamism in the list, the number of stocks traded on the Amex rose from 880 on January 1, 1960 to 1,419 on December 31, 1972. To achieve this net gain of 539 stocks required the Exchange to list 1,566 new issues. The reason it was necessary to list all these new stocks in order to achieve such a relatively small net change lies in the fact that for one reason or another stocks are continuously being dropped from the list.

The reasons for these delistings as they are called falls into three broad categories, the most numerous of which stems from the merger of one listed company into some other concern. Thus a company's own success and attractiveness often causes it to become an acquisition target. The success of these merger and acquisition attempts resulted in a loss to Amex of 350 companies.

Next, the Exchange lost 308 stocks not because of their success but because of difficulties they could not overcome. These 308 stocks were delisted because they no longer met Amex standards for continued listing. The underlying philosophy here is that for a stock to continue to be listed, the company must demonstrate its ability to remain a viable business enterprise with a large and interested public following of shareholders.

Under this view, whenever the net tangible assets of a company drop below $2 million or when a concern loses money for two of its most recent years, the Exchange begins to consider if perhaps delisting is appropriate. Even before this, if a company's assets fall below $4 million it becomes a delisting candidate.

Stocks also may be delisted when the number of publicly held shares shrinks below 200,000; when the total number of shareholders drops below 600; when the number of round lot holders drops below 400 or when the market value of the publicly held stock is less than $1 million. When stocks fall in this category, they generally have so little stock in public hands that it is impossible for the specialist to provide a good auction market for the stock. For such inactive stocks the best market is the over-the-counter market where dealers are permitted wider markups in order to permit them to cover the added expense in inventorying such stocks profitably.

Another 66 issues mostly bonds and preferred stocks were delisted during this period generally because they either had been redeemed or conversions had dwindled the supply down to where a market no longer existed.

Larry takes these losses philosophically because he knows they are unavoidable. But the losses that sting are the 301 stocks that transferred to the New York Stock Exchange. From the specialist's economic standpoint, these stocks are very important.

Therefore, the shift of trading to the New York Stock Exchange is a most serious problem because it drains a unit of its most profitable, most prestigious stocks. The alert specialist does what he can to slow down this tendency to transfer by providing the finest markets possible. Nevertheless, the basis of the shift is historical and difficult to reverse.

Insofar as brokers doing business with the public are concerned it does not matter where a stock trades because they generally have memberships on both exchanges. Thus they can continue to serve their clients regardless of where the stock is traded. But to a specialist the loss of a stock can trigger an economic crisis for him, sometimes of such gravity that it is difficult to provide effective markets in his remaining stocks.

Thus a specialist must learn to accept not only unforseen market risks but also the constant threat of losing his most profitable income producers. Most have learned to survive in this difficult atmosphere. Nevertheless, they bitterly resent the inequity in their relative position noting that Big Board specialists are not under similar pressure because if a N.Y.S.E. specialist fails to perform, "Where the hell can the company go?"

Nothing brings out the worst in a specialist than the suggestion that a company is leaving because of poor specialist performance.

"This is simply not true," claims Larry. "We make tighter markets, we provide greater depth, and we keep the spreads between trades narrower. We have to, that is the only leverage we have. Often when a company finds that their stock does seem to have a better market after it leaves us, what they fail to take into consideration is that just before moving to the Big Board they either split their stock or had a secondary stock offering. They do this because to list on the Big Board a company has to have a greater number of shares outstanding as well as more stockholders than we accept as a minimum. The greater the number of shareholders and outstanding shares, the easier it is to make a good market. Therefore, what happens is that by issuing more shares it eliminates the condition which caused the difficult market in the first place.

"Frankly, I think a lot of the criticism specialists get both here and on the Big Board is due to the fact that nobody likes to see stocks go down in price. Nobody complains when prices go up. Nobody complains when a company invests big dollars in a big public relations effort to make its stock better known in order for its price to rise. But everyone blames us when the promises don't work out causing the price to fall.

"We don't set the price. All those people out there trading the stock do that. Any time the price of a stock gets too far out of line, people are free to exploit these disparities if they choose to.

"Another thing that works against us is the ignorance of most people as to the nature of stock price movements; they don't realize what

large investments we often have in a stock during periods its performance is most visibly poor. As a result, we often have to invest more of
our capital in positions than we might care to make. This means we
have bigger risks."

In order to receive his share of new stocks, Larry carefully reads the
weekly bulletin issued by the Exchange Secretary. This bulletin lists
all companies that have formally applied for an Amex listing. A company's application is approved after it has gone through an extensive
formal listing process. This involves a screening process to determine
that there is nothing in the background of either the company or its
principals that might be embarrassing or detrimental and that the
company fully meets the Exchange's requirements for listing.

At the same time, stockholder lists are reviewed and its over-the-
counter market is studied to verify that the company is likely to be
helped rather than hurt by a potential exchange listing.

Assuming that the issue is fully qualified, it is approved for listing
by the Board at one of its regular Thursday meetings. On the day
following approval, a fact sheet and a copy of the company's detailed
listing application is distributed to each specialist unit.

After reading this material, any specialist interested in handling the
stock submits his request to the Exchange's Allocation Department.
At the same time, if a company has any specific specialist requests,
the Exchange's Listing Representative working with the company will
pass the company's request along to the allocations committee.

Specialist applications for each stock are closed about a week before
the allocations committee assigns the stock. In the interim period, the
staff puts together for the committee a dossier on all the specialists
applying for each stock approved for listing that week. This dossier
contains the names of every specialist unit applying for each stock.
Among other things, it contains a summary of the arguments each
specialist has made as to why the commitee should assign the stock to
him, a data sheet on the company, and information about each of the
bidding specialist units.

Included in this package is a list of the stocks handled by each unit.
This shows not only the name of each company but the type of business the company is engaged in. The idea here is that if a specialist
already handles more than one stock in a given industry preference
will be given to some other unit to prevent any significant industry
concentration.

A second list shows all the stocks allocated to and lost by each unit during the previous 2 years. This list shows not only the dates on which the most recent issues were acquired and lost but also reasons for any losses. For instance, if a specialist lost a stock because poor performance on his part caused the stock to be allocated to another specialist unit this will work against the specialist in his bid for new stocks.

Each specialist's record of performance is analyzed on an individual basis, stock by stock and collectively for all the stocks in his unit. This collective performance record is then compared to the over-all average performance of all exchange specialists in all stock issues. To the extent that his performance is better than average, this is a plus factor; if his performance is poorer than average it is likely to be detrimental to his application unless the specialist can show his poor performance was due to extenuating circumstances.

Each applicant's most recent financial statements are also submitted. If a stock is likely to be a large financial burden on a specialist initially, the committee will attempt to allocate the stock to the applying unit best able to take a loss a the present time. If it appears likely that a stock will not need an extensive seasoning period, it is likely to be given to a specialist who is not doing well in order to bolster his earnings.

A record of any complaints made against a specialist, the nature of the complaint and its disposition is made available to the committee. They also have at their disposal a chronological list of the stocks most recently admitted to trading and the units to which these stocks were assigned.

All the information is forwarded to the Allocations Committee each week there are stocks to be allocated, to assist them in making the actual selection. The committee consists of two governors who are specialists, three who are brokers, three from members' firm offices and one who is a Senior Floor Official. As you can see this committee is weighed heavily in favor of brokers and office governors, not specialists.

Because the committee is composed as it is, it behooves each specialist unit not only maintain a statistically good performance but at the same time to maintain as cordial a relationship with broker members as possible despite their adversary roles in the auction process. A specialist who is too abrasive in his dealings with brokers will soon find that the Allocations Committee is made aware of the fact and only the less attractive listings will be assigned to him.

This particular committee composition was arrived at in an effort to resolve the abuses which allegedly occurred in the allocation process prior to the reorganization in 1962. In those days the Committee was supposed to have been composed of a more or less permanent group of specialists who were reported to have allocated stocks on the basis of loyalty to the ruling clique.

As each new stock comes up for consideration, members of the committee are supposed to nominate those specialists they think best qualified to handle the stock based on the statistical information they have. When all the nominations are closed and the discussion completed, the committee members defer to the Exchange Secretary who is in attendance at each meeting. If it turns out that one of the specialists nominated happens to be one of the company's choices, this fact is now made known.

If, however, the company requested a specialist who for some reason either did not apply for the stock or who was not nominated , the Secretary makes no mention of this fact. Instead he just passes. After the Secretary's comments, if any, additional discussion may take place as to why the company should or should not get the specialist of its choice.

When all discussion is completed the committee is ready to vote. If no specialist receives a majority of the votes on the first ballot, the specialist with the fewest votes is eliminated and a new vote will be taken. Voting continues for as many rounds as necessary to secure a majority vote for the successful unit.

Larry believes that bidding for new stocks is a science all to itself. "If you bid for everything," he says, "they give you the stocks that no one else wants. Then when a real winner comes along the committee turns you down pointing to the stocks they allocated to you in the recent past."

In the belief that good specialist units, as a matter of confidence and loyalty to the Exchange should bid as a matter of course on the less desirable stocks, Larry once bid on virtually every marginal issue that was listed over a period of several months. However, he saw that this was going to be prejudicial to his unit so he reluctantly abandoned this policy.

In addition to bidding on some potentially difficult stocks in order to qualify for the potential plums, there is another technique Larry uses when applying for the more attractive stocks. He notes that the committee is more amenable to applications when a unit's commission income is down or when its increase is below average as compared to the other units. As a result, he puts in for more stocks when his income is off a bit and holds back from applying when his commission income is relatively high.

"If the committee sees you are making what they consider to be too much money, they pass you by figuring someone else could use the income to better advantage than you can. Therefore, it pays to be more selective at some times than at others.

"I usually expect to get about one out of each ten stocks I apply for. Once my acceptance ratio gets below that figure, I generally wait until a particularly attractive stock is approved. Sometimes this works, sometimes it doesn't."

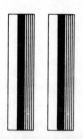

Similarities and Differences — Exchange vs. Over-the-Counter

ALTHOUGH the forces propelling price movements are exactly the same in both cases, there is a fundamental difference in the price setting mechanism as it operates on an Exchange and in the so-called Over-the-Counter market. This difference stems from the fact that an Exchange market is an auction market where an investor through his agent is often able to trade directly with his public counterpart. In contrast, the agent of an investor purchasing an over-the-counter stock must virtually always purchase it from a dealer.

The name, dealer, implies that anyone who acts as one carries an inventory of whatever it is that he is selling. Thus a dealer in stocks is a person who carries an inventory of stock which he buys at one price and hopes to resell at a higher price. The difference between what the dealer (or anyone else) is willing to buy or sell stock at, at any particular moment is called the spread. One side of the spread is the bid. This is the highest price a dealer or another investor will pay for your stock if you want to sell. The other side is the offer or the price you must pay if you want to buy.

When an investor trades over-the-counter, he invariably buys from or sells to the dealer. Thus, if the dealer is quoting a stock at 14–14½ and two investors are both interested in a stock at about the same time, one looking to buy and the other looking to sell, the dealer will buy from one party at 14, then immediately turn around and sell it to the other at 14½. On an exchange, however, if both orders were to reach the floor at the same time, the difference would probably be split and the buyer's order would be offset against the seller's at 14¼. Thus, each investor saves himself a ¼ point or 25 cents per share on the trade.

On the Exchanges, investors looking to buy or sell usually have their orders offset directly with other public orders about 85 per cent of the time. The rest of the time they effect their trade wih the specialist who acts in much the same capacity as the over-the-counter dealer. By trading directly with their public counterparts in the majority of cases the price to the investor is generally more favorable.

Another significant difference lies in the nature of the Over-the-Counter market. Because of its huge size and the physical dispersion of its trading facilities, the O-T-C market cannot be as closely monitored as an Exchange market. As a result, it is possible for trades to take place at virtually the same time but through different dealers at widely different prices. The growing acceptance of the Over-the-Counter NASDAQ quotation system is minimizing the disparities but they continue to exist. On an Exchange in contrast, because all interest is expressed in one place, each trade always takes place at the best available price of that moment. As evidence that the cost of trading O-T-C stocks is higher than the cost of doing business on an exchange, many brokers pay their registered representatives double the exchange commission rate on all O-T-C orders.

The amount saved by trading a stock listed on an exchange is the amount of markup the dealer has to charge in order to cover the expense of carrying the stock in his inventory. Since transactions on the Amex involve the specialist acting as a dealer in about only 15 per cent of all cases, the aggregate amount of dealer markup charged to investors using the facilities of an exchange is a fraction of what a comparable volume of transactions would cost in the over-the-counter market.

A broker who enters an O-T-C order first consults what is known as the NASDAQ quotation console at his firm. This is an electronic machine that looks like a 12 or 14 inch television set with a typewriter keyboard attached to it. By punching the correct keys on the typewriter, the names of all brokers who have set themselves up as dealers in the stock appear on the television screen.

The names are arranged in two different ways, according to whether a broker is looking to buy or sell. Since our broker is looking to buy, he presses the keyboard to show him the dealers in order from the one offering stock at the lowest price to the one offering at the highest price.

He then calls the dealer making the best offer to negotiate the transaction for his customer. Prices on the over-the-counter market constantly change just as they do on the exchanges. Therefore, the price our broker actually negotiates with the dealer may differ from the price shown on the screen. It's not supposed to differ because it takes only a few seconds to change a quote but frequent changes do occur at times.

When the price negotiated is less favorable than the price quoted on the console, a good broker will attempt to determine whether this was due to an actual change in the market for the stock or whether the favorable quote was merely a tactic employed by the dealer to gain the most favorable position on the quote machine. Some dealers are said to make favorable quotes with the idea that once they induce a broker to call them, they can then "back off" from their quote and attempt to negotiate a trade at a less favorable price. This tactic has been one of the more serious problems with which the National Association of Securities Dealers has had to deal. It may continue to be a problem until such time as the O-T-C market extends its automation to the point where a broker will be able to "lock in" his order to the quotation being advertised.

Under current O-T-C rules of practice, all quotes in the NASDAQ console are supposed to be firm prices for any trade up to 100 shares after which the dealer is free to complete the order at another higher "clean up" price. This is similar to the practice on an exchange when the specialist is required to act as a dealer.

Once he has negotiated the transaction a broker has two options. He can act as an agent on the order or he can act as principal. If he acts as agent, he bills the customer at exactly the price he paid for the stock from the O-T-C dealer, then charges him a commission for executing the order. If he decides to do the trade as a dealer, he adds a "markup" to the price he paid the O-T-C dealer and then bills his customer this higher price, "net," without charging an additional commission. The higher price is supposed to include his profit in handling the order for his customer. It is considered unethical, perhaps illegal as well, for the broker to charge a commission on top of his markup.

Doing business over the counter is a little bit like buying a used car in that while there are a number of approximate guidelines that can be followed in making a deal there are few fixed rules that investors may rely on. Through his broker and his broker's NASDAQ television screen, the investor "shops the street" looking for the dealer who will offer him the best deal. When he finds someone, his broker then has to contact the dealer and negotiate with him to make sure that the deal is as good as it looks.

An exchange auction market, on the other hand, is a market where individual investors enter their orders (again through their brokers) directly into one central market place. Here the competing orders of everyone interested in the stock are "on the table" as it were, and they interact in such a manner that a stock always sells at its most favorable price.

On an exchange every order that anyone in the world has placed is forwarded to the post of the specialist assigned the stock. In this manner everyone interested in a stock is able to enter his bid. Only the most favorable prices of the moment have any relevance. Only the most favored prices are quoted. Therefore, whatever the price of the moment, regardless of how unfair the price might seem to someone, the investor at least knows that he can accept it or reject it without concerning himself with whether or not he might be able to get a better price from someone else at that particular point in time.

Because investors on an exchange market have the opportunity to compete with all other investors, they are able to consummate transactions directly with investors in the great majority of cases. However, an investor using the over-the-counter market rarely if ever does so. An investor who buys or sells stock over the counter almost always buys it from or sells it to a dealer who maintains an inventory in the stock.

The more often a dealer interjects himself into a securities transaction, the more the investor in the aggregate will have to pay for his securities because the warehousing function that dealers provide, of necessity builds into the transaction expenses which a person using the dealer's facilities must pay for. The dealer must concern himself with the cost of maintaining his inventory, operating expenses of his staff and equipment as well as a hoped for profit for his efforts.

Because of the necessity of funneling all O-T-C orders through a dealer, both the buyer and seller are likely to receive a less favorable price on the execution of their orders than if it were possible to cross their orders directly as on an exchange.

A simple way to illustrate this is to look at the first 10 over-the-counter stocks listed in the *Wall Street Journal* on November 24, 1971.

	Bid	**Asked**
A.A.I. Corp.	7½	8
Aberle Industries	1	1¼
Accelerators, Inc.	7	7½
Ace Industries	4	4⅜
Acme Electric	7	7⅜
Acushnet Corp.	21½	22¼
ADA Financial	4¼	5¼
Addison Wesley	13¼	14⅝
Adley Corp.	5⅛	5⅝
ADM Industries	9⅞	10¼

Although it may not be a representative situation, nevertheless, ADA Financial illustrates in an extreme way the problem of investing over-the-counter. If a buyer and seller were to make a trade simultaneously, the buyer would have to pay 5¼ while at the same time the seller was receiving only 4¼, perhaps from the same dealer. Not only are these executions unsatisfactory from both the buyer and seller's point of view, but the variation between the two transactions occurring simultaneously is a full point or 24 per cent of the bid price.

On the other hand, if both orders had met head-on in the Exchange auction market, there is a good chance that if the auction process was effectively at work the trade would have taken place at about the midpoint, 4¾. By meeting in this manner both buyer and seller each save a ½ point and the spread between individual trades is considerably narrowed. Instead of possible successive swings of a full point between trades as buyers, then sellers come into the market, the variation between prices on an exchange between consecutive trades in this price category would seldom be more than ⅛ point.

Although the exchange auction market thus permits buy and sell orders to directly offset each other whenever possible, if no buyer is present when a sell order appears, or vice versa, the specialist assigned to the stock is required to step in and act as a dealer so that trades can occur. When this happens, he functions much as an over-the-counter dealer would. However, unlike the NASD dealer, an Amex specialist acting for his own account must trade at a price that bears a close and reasonable relationship to the activity which immediately preceded it. Because of the centralization of orders on an exchange, it is relatively simple to insure that the specialist does indeed function as required.

In acting either as a principal for his own account or as an agent for someone else, the specialist must insure that price continuity in his stocks is maintained. That is, as the price level of a stock changes in response to market pressures, he has to see to it that the level of change is gradual from one trade to the next.

Over-the-counter, the pressure of immediate market trading does not necessarily act so precisely on a stock for two reasons. First of all the spread is usually much wider allowing the dealer a greater profit margin on most transactions. Because of this greater profit margin, the O-T-C dealer sometimes appears to offer a stock greater stability than a specialist. For instance, on November 8, 1971 ADA Financial was quoted in the *Wall Street Journal* at 3½–5. At this quote, a dealer could almost break even if he just sold 200 shares for every 300 shares he bought. He could then afford to hold those remaining 100 shares almost indefinitely until the market strengthened. By not changing the quote, the stock might appear to be more stable than a listed stock which also traded in a range between 3½ and 5 for weeks on end but whose day to day price change might be as much as ½ point per day.

If an O-T-C dealer sees his market going against him or even likely to go against him, he can adjust his quotations either up or down in such a way as not to be competitive with other dealers. He can anticipate market conditions and change his quotes accordingly, even before the actual pressure of market orders force a change in the price level. Other dealers seeing what is happening may sometimes follow suit, the effect being that the entire quoting range has changed even though no actual business was transacted.

Since there is no satisfactory mechanism to regulate them on a continuous basis, market makers may often refuse to deal in stocks when they feel market conditions are unfavorable. One such example of this occurred in November, 1971 when an important dealer who had been making markets in about 500 O-T-C stocks announced that he would no longer quote markets in 200 of his stocks. Presumably these were his least profitable issues.

The effect of this decision on his part may have left some of these 200 companies and their investors without any market making mechanism. In such extreme cases, under very unfavorable market conditions, if a stock were to lose its market makers, a stockholder would be left with absolutely no mechanism through which to trade his stock because O-T-C market makers are not under the same affirmative obligation to trade stocks as are exchange specialists.

On an exchange, each transaction is printed on a stock ticker tape usually within a minute after it occurs. At the end of the day newspapers all over the country print the exact volume of transactions and the exact range of prices at which trades took place. On the following day, stock exchange record rooms and independent statistical services make available to those who need or want to know it, a complete record of each and every transaction, its price and the exact time it occurred. On the over-the-counter market, at the current time, none of this information can be known with precision. Because of technical problems associated with the reporting procedures used in the O-T-C market, volume as it is reported for any stocks serves only to show relative activity while reported quotations show only the approximate price range at which transactions have taken place.

12

The Day the Bottom Fell Out

IF THERE is one thing the stock market has no use for, it is a surprise. There is no way to anticipate surprises or to discount them in the price structure. Surprises of any kind invariably confuse the market. Unfortunately, confused markets are often down markets.

One such surprise in recent years came as a result of a military confrontation in the Middle East.

For the market, it could not have come at a worse time. The market had been doing well for almost 9 months and people were beginning to think the market was going to go up forever. Of course it wasn't going to go up forever. It never does. Already there were signs that it was getting a little bit tired. One could sense that the early buyers were using the underlying strength of the market to feed their stock out to the late-comers to lock in capital gains before there was too much competition.

Now with the news, there was going to be a new ball game. The "Johnny come latelys" were all going to run for cover at once. Not only were they not going to be buying anything this morning but the more

70

nervous among them would also be dumping stock indiscriminately in a futile attempt to keep their losses down.

Consequently, Larry had to resign himself to the fact that he was going to have to buy a lot of stock today, most of which he would prefer to pass up. But, of course, he was not going to have any choice in the matter.

Riding to the Exchange this morning, his paper went unread. He didn't even glance at the sports page to see how last night's Mets game turned out. Instead his mind seemed to be miles away as he stared blankly out of the window of the "galloping commuter." If he were interested he would have noted that his train was 20 minutes late but that wouldn't bother him today.

Instead, his computerlike mind is busy scanning his brain for all the data it has on each of the stocks in the unit's book. Apex? No trouble here. Fortunately, he went short 7,200 shares on a 15,000 share block late last week. After the trade he became a little uneasy about how he was going to cover. He really stuck his neck out by accommodating that buyer but now maybe there'll be a chance to even up his position.

World Wide? Larry doesn't have to worry here either. Someone has been buying the stock every time it was weak for the last 2 years. Whoever it is must be covering his tracks well. He's got to have enough stock by now to demand a seat on World Wide's board of directors but there haven't been any new directors for the past 5 years. Larry sometimes wonders what the game is here but today he doesn't care. If the stock is weak, he knows support will appear and for this he is grateful.

Midland? No problem here either. The stock is never really active no matter what happens. There is a small inventory. Not enough to worry about. So long as volume today stays low, the unit can absorb all the selling that comes in.

Hartford? This could be a problem but then there is a good book on the buy side. If only they don't cancel their bids before the opening, everything should be all right.

Muncy? That's a ticket writer. No problem here unless the crisis takes a turn for the worse. Anything bought here today can be turned over to the bargain hunters in a day or two. Actually, if things work out well there ought to be 2 or 3 points in the stock to compensate for the trouble.

Twinkle? Now here's a sticky number! Twinkle has been the big stock for over a year but the handwriting is already on the wall. After moving from 25 to 125, the play in Twinkle is coming to a close. Several months back the company split its stock and just last Friday there was a big secondary. Some of the money went to the company but most of the stock came from insiders bailing out. They distributed better than a half million shares. But the issue was sticky and the underwriter was having trouble peddling it. In fact, the underwriter still had some stock on the shelf. This stock was overhanging the market with the underwriter trying to feed it out at every opportunity.

Consequently, there could be some real trouble because here is a stock that everyone has a reason to sell. The stock ran up so strongly in the past 6 months that any long-term holder could sell the extra shares he received on the split for more than his original investment. Anyone in this category who was the least bit nervous was likely to sell in order to lock in his capital gains. Who could blame him? But this would not solve Larry's problem. He knew only too well that underwriters make their money from the commissions they get selling stock to others, not by investing in stocks at retail prices for their own account. Therefore, if the underwriter was stuck with stock, he was going to be active dumping what he couldn't sell last week.

At the same time, except for day traders and scalpers, Larry couldn't see where any substantial buying was going to come from. Anyone who ever wanted to buy Twinkle already had more than adequate opportunity to do so. If by chance there might have been someone around who never heard of the stock, the underwriter's salesman should have taken care of that last Friday as they looked into every possible nook and cranny to find the investors to whom to sell the secondary.

He didn't bother going to his office this morning but instead went directly down to the post. Two partners were already there. The buzz of activity was greater than normal and his clerk was busy at work setting up the books and matching orders to be ready for the opening.

As soon as he reached the post Larry picked up the book in Twinkle and started flipping through the tickets.

Last Friday, the stock closed at 41. Luckily he finished the week carrying a nominal inventory of only 115 shares. At the close he had an order to buy 5,000 shares at 40 along with small amounts of stock at various prices down to 38. He was relieved to find the 40 bid still there but this relief was short-lived. Within minutes of reaching the post, the broker who entered the order cancelled it.

Several smaller orders to buy were also cancelled. Replacement buy orders were sparse. One bargain hunter came in with an order to buy 500 TNK at 38⅝ while orders to buy at the market totaled 700 shares. All told Larry had orders to buy a total of 4,400 shares at various prices down to $38 per share.

While the buy side of the book was light, the sell side rang loud and clear as to the kind of day this was going to be. There were orders to sell over 15,000 shares and even before the opening, a crowd was beginning to form at the post. By the time the market opened, Larry was faced with orders to sell over 25,000 shares!

The gong rang. It was ten o'clock. Another market day had started. He gritted his teeth. His nails dug into the palm of his hands, already sweating even though he had yet to make his first trade. His stomach tightened and his mind, sharper, quicker, and more accurate than any computer I. B. M. ever designed, mentally scanned his Twinkle orders for the last time. What he saw was the group of orders summarized on page 74.

He saw that the smallest opening he could possibly arrange would be 3,700 shares because there were 3,700 shares to sell at the market.

At what prices should Twinkle open?

The rules of the Exchange say a specialist is not to change the direction of the market whenever he buys or sells stock for his own account. Since the stock last sold at 41 on a downtick, a trade at 41⅛ would constitute a change of trend. It would be sheer suicide to open the stock at 41⅛ or better because at that price everyone on his book who wanted to sell stock, would receive an opening price of 41⅛. On the other hand, since the only people willing to buy at this price are the buyers of the 700 shares at the market, this would mean that Larry would have to buy the remaining 25,000 shares for his own account. In a weak market, with sellers predominating, this would entail an investment of over $1 million for an act that would not only prove economically unprofitable but might also cause Larry to be censured as well.

Because so many people want to sell stock and in fact are willing to sell at prices lower than 41⅛, the effect of this action would be to change the direction of the market in an upward direction in the face of pressure dictating that it should open lower. When he buys or sells for himself, the one thing a specialist should not do is change the direction of the market.

The next thing he is forbidden to do is to trade unnecessarily for

Twinkle, Inc. (TNK)
Status of Specialist's Book at the
Opening of Trading

Orders to Buy	Price	Orders to Sell
700	Market	3,700
	41⅛ and above	6,700
200	41	5,200
	40¾	3,300
	40⅝	400
500	40½	1,800
	40¼	300
300	40⅛	900
400	40	3,400
600	39⅞	
400	39½	
300	39	
700	38⅝	
100	38½	
200	38	

his own account. Each trade he makes has to be reasonably necessary in view of the market conditions at hand. For him to buy 25,000 shares of stock, most of it at prices above what sellers are willing to accept as a fair price would not only be foolish but in the eyes of the Exchange an unnecessary transaction.

Finally for a specialist to buy over $1 million worth of stock on an opening trade would be sheer idiocy because he knows that as the day proceeds, he is going to need that money to provide support not only for Twinkle but for other stocks as well.

If 41⅛ is out, how about 41? This will knock out the 6,700 shares to sell at 41⅛ or better and it will pick up buy orders for 200 shares at 41. His equation at this point will be 900 shares to buy versus 19,000 shares to sell. To complete this trade, Larry would have to buy 18,100 shares. This is also too much stock to buy.

How about 40¾? Here we knock out both the 6,700 shares to sell at 41⅛ and the 5,200 to sell at 41. That leaves 13,800 shares to sell against 900 to buy. Larry would have to buy 8,600 shares which he still considers too much.

He goes down his orders in this manner until he gets to 39⅞. At 39⅞, he has knocked every limit order to sell on his book out. All he has left are those orders to sell the 3,700 shares at the market. Offsetting this, he has bunched together the orders to buy 700 shares at the market, 200 shares at 41, 500 shares at 40½, 300 at 40⅛, 400 at 40 and 600 at 39⅞. These buy orders total 2,700 shares. At 39⅞, Larry has to buy only 1,000 shares for his own account.

He could conceivably drop the stock to 39½ and just buy 600 shares; or to 39 and buy 300 shares or even 38⅝ and not buy any stock at all. But his job is to try to balance all the conflicting forces at work in a stock as equitably as possible. Too low an opening might trigger a panic, putting much more stock on the market than is already going to trade and he doesn't want that to happen. Too big a gap in the opening price will also call in the house detectives from the Exchange's market operations areas who supervise trading in the markets. They have some pretty sticky ideas concerning the market and might cause Larry to be censured if they thought the opening was too low.

He feels he can justify a drop of a point and an eighth under the prevailing market conditions this morning so he strikes the opening price at 39⅞.

"3,700 TNK opens at 39⅞" he shouts.

The Exchange reporter quickly scribbles this on his pad, tears off the sheet, time stamps it and hands it to a clerk inside the post. The clerk immediately enters the details of the order on an electronic keyboard and transmits it to the ticker computer. Within 15 seconds after entering and transmitting the data, tickers throughout the world carry the news that Twinkle opened on 3,700 shares at 39⅞.

It is appropriate to note here that whether the buyers at the opening were willing to buy at the market, at 41 or at 39⅞, they all received the benefit of the 39⅞ price. This was the best available price at the opening and therefore everyone who was willing to buy at this price or higher received the benefit of the 39⅞ opening price.

Sellers on the other hand who entered orders to sell at 41 would not have their orders executed at 39⅞ because 39⅞ is less favorable than the minimum price they said they were willing to accept. Before their orders can be executed, the stock will have to sell up to at least 41, the price they stated was their lowest offering price.

As quickly as Larry announced the opening trade and handed the executed orders to his clerk, he noted that the next highest bid price was 39½ where he had orders to buy 400 shares. The lowest price at which he had orders to sell was 40. At 40, Larry had orders to sell 3,400 shares. This made his actual public quote 39½ bid–40 offered–last sale 39⅞.

However, because another of Larry's obligations is to minimize fluctuations in the price of the stock from one trade to the next, he decides to step ahead of the 39½ bid with a bid of his own at 39⅝.

Instead of permitting the stock to drop possibly ⅜ point on the next trade if it is a trade initiated by a seller, his bid will limit the drop to ¼ point. If the next person who enters a market order in Twinkle wants to sell, the stock will trade at 39⅝, down ¼. On the other hand, if the next order will be an order to buy at the market, Twinkle will trade at 40, up ⅛ from the 39⅞ trade.

Larry barely manages to open his other stocks when the activity in Twinkle warms up in earnest.

"How's TNK?"

"39⅝–40."

"Sell 100."

"You've got it. Harkins, Leifer #101."

A broker came in with an order to sell 100 shares of TNK at the market. After asking for the quotation, he accepts the bid for his customer and sells 100 shares at 39⅝. Larry confirmed the trade by telling the broker that the buyer was his firm, Harkins, Leifer & Company. This means that the specialist purchased the stock for his own account. At the same time, he gave the broker his clearing number, #101, so that the broker's back office would know where to deliver the stock.

After this transaction, the best public bid is still 39½ and his best public offer is still 40. The next broker asks,

"How's TNK?"

"39½–⅞," says Larry after again tightening the market by offering to sell from his inventory at 39⅞ instead of at the public offer of 40.

"What's the size."

"400 by 100."

"Sell 500 at the half."

"You've got it. Buy 400 Bear Brothers, #115; 100 Harkins, Leifer, #101."

The broker asked for a quote and found it to be 39½ bid–39⅞ offered. Since he had more than 100 shares to sell, he asked for the size. On hearing that the specialist had orders to buy 400 at 39½, he placed his order to sell 500 shares at that price. Larry had an option at this point of selling 400 shares at the 39½ bid and placing a 100 share open order to sell on his book at 39½ or of picking up the remaining 100 shares for himself. He chose to do the latter thereby tightening up the market in the process by adding that remaining 100 shares into his inventory.

The orders to sell kept coming in. To try to ease the decline Larry bought additional stock at 39⅜, 39⅛, 39 and 38⅞ before hitting into a small pocket of demand for 700 shares at 38⅝.

It was not until 10:32 that the first signs of bargain hunting appeared as someone came in to buy 100 shares at the market. By this time 8,100 shares had already traded, all on down ticks and Larry had bought over 3,700 shares for his own account. When buyers began to nibble, Larry was able to sell off about 500 shares before another wave of selling hit the market.

Again he took in stock at 38½, 38⅜, 38⅛, 38, 37¾. Once again a few small buyers nibbled, but sellers with limit orders have been following the stock down. Their overhanging orders prevent any substantial rally. As before, the buying dried up so quickly it was almost as though it was never there. Again he bought 100 at 37¾, 300 at 37⅝, 100 at 37½, 200 at 37½, 100 at 37, 400 at 36¾, 800 at 36⅜, 200 at 36⅛ and 100 at 36⅛.

"Damn it all," he wondered. "Where is the bottom? When will all this selling stop?" His position is now up to 5,873 shares and he still has no evidence of any support. "How low do I have to let prices drop," he asks himself, "before someone other than me is going to want to buy? After all, this is supposed to be a two-way auction market, isn't it? Where in hell are all the buyers?"

There are always supposed to be both buyers and sellers in every market and they are supposed to trade at prices that are mutually acceptable to each. The specialist is only supposed to be there when temporary disparities develop. He's not supposed to stand there and buy all the stock.

Then, for a brief instant all activity on the floor seemed to stop. There was a split second of absolute silence. From out of this silence a cry went up. A swell of noise as powerful as any material force anyone has ever encountered starts to rise in intensity. Almost in one voice, everyone on the Floor begins to chorus, "The market's rallying! It's rallying!"

For someone who never has been on the floor of a stock exchange, the activity that builds up from this base of silence is at once awe-inspiring, and unbelievable. There is an invisible wave of excitement that strikes with a force you not only can hear but feel and smell as well, as it rolls over you and engulfs you in its sweep. Where first there was activity and noise, there descends an absolute, dead silence almost as overwhelming as the formless silence described in Genesis. From this silence there comes a new activity; an activity that brings with it a new noise—the noise of enthusiasm, the noise of a market going up. And, now such a moment of truth arrived!

Where just a minute before, it was all sell, sell, sell. Now it was all buy, buy, buy. Larry scents the change and he is ready! He sells 200 at 36⅜, 300 at 36⅝, 100 at 36⅞. "Damn it, there is someone with a limit order to sell at 37. Sell his stock quick! Get that sell order out of the way." There was lots of stock to sell and Larry wanted out from under as much as possible at as high a price as possible. Just in case the rally did not last, Larry wanted to come as close to evening out his position as he could.

The stock was back up to 37¾ very quickly. Between 37¾ and 38 there were so many orders on his book that Larry didn't get a chance to lighten his own inventory for about an hour and a half. Then during the last hour of trading, temporary gaps on both sides of the market appeared, necessitating him both to buy and sell for his own account to keep the market orderly.

At the end of the day, Twinkle closed as 37⅞, down 3⅛ points from the previous close on round lot volume of 30,800 plus an additional 2,804 odd lot shares. During this day Larry purchased 13,196 shares while managing to resell only 8,408 shares. This left him with a net long position of over 4,900 shares. His activity made him an important factor both as a buyer or seller in 64 per cent of all round lot trades during the day. This is an abnormally high percentage of participation. But what he did was necessary to prevent utter chaos from engulfing the stock.

As it was, the performance of the stock did not look too good from the raw data that appeared in the papers.

Twinkle did drop almost 12 per cent from Friday's 41 to a low of 36⅛ in just one day. Actually the decline did not take a full day but just one hour and forty three minutes. On the surface it appeared as though Larry had abandoned the stock to fend for itself.

Yet, as we have seen, this was not the case. If it had not been for the specialist, the stock would have been down to 38 by 10:09 at which time all the buy orders on his book would have been exhausted. After that the stock might not have traded until new buyers could have been found, most likely at prices much lower than 36⅛. However, because of Larry's activities, the stock at 10:09 was trading not at 38 but at 39⅛, a full point and an eighth higher.

Instead of walking away from the market, Larry had used a total of over $500,000 of his firm's money to buy stock in an effort to bring order out of chaos at a time when chaos seemed imminent. On the way down to 36⅛, 39 of 53 trades occurred because someone had been panicked into selling by the news of the previous day and the effect they thought this news would have on the market. By becoming frightened and selling, these investors, in effect, created for themselves a self-fulfilling prophecy. This irrational panic was costly not only to the investors but to Larry as well because the trading he was obligated to do resulted in a trading loss that day of almost $1,100 on completed trades.

The stock he bought cost him an average of $38.12 per share while he was able to resell the 8,408 shares for only $37.99 per share. This gave him a loss of about 13 cents per share or about $1,100. In addition to this, he had to pay interest charges on the remaining inventory overnight plus transfer taxes on the shares he sold, thus raising his loss for the day even more.

The shares held over at the end of the day carried a further potential loss of about $1,225 because the closing price for the day (37⅞) was less than the average purchase price.

The specialist's biggest loss, however, comes not in dollars but in the form of undeserved criticism from people who think it is the specialist who masterminds these drops in price for his own profit. They generally do not bother to give general market conditions or the technical condition of the stock itself any credit (or blame) for the move. For those interested in details, the complete journal of activity for this day showing the specialist's round lot purchases and sales is included as Appendix A at the end of this book, while a summary of both round lot and odd lot specialist activity by price is included as Appendix B.

It should be noted that this type of trading pattern is not typical of what happens to most stocks on most days. It is, however, typical of what very often happens on days when unexpected news hits the market. These are the days when unexpected calamities cause stocks to drop rapidly in price.

An example like this should prove that, although specialists may not consciously concern themselves with larger public service issues, the faithful adherence to their obligations on such days automatically adjusts their behavior to serving the larger public good whether or not in the end they profit from any single transaction or series of trades.

As the market opened on this day it was evident that the stock was going to drop and drop sharply. If he were the sole determinant of his personal trading activity, he undoubtedly would have stepped aside and not bought anything at the opening or during the early part of the trading sequence. The trade by trade summary accompanying this book in Appendix A shows he did no such thing, but instead stayed in there buying and providing solid market support until the wave of selling had exhausted itself.

Each share that he bought at any price above 36⅛ represented stock that he might possibly have purchased at a lower price if he were truly accountable to no one but himself. Knowing as he did that selling pressure was driving the stock lower and lower, this would have been the most profitable course of action to follow.

This illustration shows dramatically that the specialist does not do what he wants to do, but instead he does what he must do to maintain an orderly market in his stocks. When studying the appendix to get an idea of how the specialist operates, observe that the trend against which the specialist buys and sells is determined from one trade to the next by market orders as they are entered by public customers. He has absolutely no control over these people, over the orders they are going to enter or the sequence in which successive buy and sell orders will be entered.

It is true that the cost of demanding instant liquidity in the market place may have been excessively high for many of the people who sold this day, especially those who sold their stock at or near the bottom at 36⅛. But as Larry will tell everyone who cares to listen, no one should ever buy or sell any stock under duress.

The Philosophy
of Specializing

WHEN WE asked Larry how much money he normally has invested in his inventory positions, he replied that there is no norm because pressures shift so unpredictably and swiftly from the buy to the sell side. However, he speculated that a position of perhaps $1 million, long or short or some combination thereof was about normal. At the bottom of the bear market in 1970, he was long as much as $5 million worth of stock. That was $5 million in real money, not Monopoly money, that the unit threw into the market to try to stem the tide at a time when it appeared that investors, and many leaders in the industry didn't think the system would survive.

"Frankly, we could not have held out more than a few days longer before we too would have run down to the end of our resources. Then, who knows what might have happened? But a successful specialist unit is often like the team that wins the ball game. As long as it can hold on to a one point lead at the one yard line when that final whistle blows, they win the game. If they can't hold out they lose everything.

"Our business is the same way. As long as we have enough buying power to buy that last 100 shares before the market turns around again we can walk away from a bear market as though it never happened. In fact, we usually come out smelling like a rose.

"We did fairly well coming out of that bear market because we had the staying power to outlast it. That's one of the keys to whipping the market. Some of the other fellows down here weren't so lucky. They didn't have either the money or the guts to outlast the deluge. Unfortunately, they were swept away. But then the market is extremely impersonal. It doesn't care who it helps or who it hurts.

"It wasn't that we wanted to buy so much, of course. If we had a choice we would have stepped aside along with everyone else. After all, no one becomes a hero by way of the bankruptcy court. But the specialist system places an obligation on us to act as buyers of last resort. If you come in with a market order and there is no one for you to trade with, we have to take the other side. We have no alternative.

"But just because I have to trade with someone doesn't mean I have to let him take advantage of me. I have no intention, for instance, of letting someone drive up one of my stocks forcing me into a huge short position, then giving him the opportunity to bail out right at the top. If someone deliberately puts me in a position where I'm going to lose money, he too will have to pay.

"I've been in this business long enough now to take on anyone who wants to play games and beat him at his own game. I'm a professional. I know my business. I think I'm as good at it as anyone can be. That's why I survive and make money at something that would break most other people."

The principal reason Larry thought he was a successful specialist was because of his ability to make rational decisions under irrational conditions. "Many, perhaps most of the reasons people use to buy and sell stocks are irrational. As a result, the market appears to outside observers to be irrational. For instance, years ago when I first came into this business the market fell sharply one day because President Eisenhower had a heart attack. That was an irrational reason for people to sell stock. It had absolutely nothing to do with fundamentals, yet many people sold. We bought lots of stock that day and turned it right around at a nice profit.

"In my own personal affairs I am not always or even often, rational. But when I'm on the Floor of this Exchange doing my job from 10:00 a.m. to 3:30 p.m. every day I am a different person. I have very few emotions. Most of my decisions are rational. Sometimes, I lose that ability and then I don't function nearly as effectively.

"Another reason we do well is because we concentrate rather than dissipate our efforts. For example, the only stocks I really follow are the stocks in our unit.

"This is my whole working life. This is all I care about. This is all I concentrate on. Should it be a surprise to anyone that I am so intimately acquainted with these stocks; that I can usually guess what is going to happen almost as soon as, or even before it happens? Should it be a surprise to anyone that I cannot only make a good public market in these stocks but at the same time make a good living for myself?

"As I said, the single most important element in determining which way the market is going to go next is psychological. Therefore, we try to determine the over-all psychological outlook of investors at any particular time.

"Invariably whenever people get hysterical about the market whether they rush to buy or sell, they are generally wrong. If you look back at the crises that affected the markets over the years they were all wrong. For instance, when President Nixon imposed wage and price controls the market went up over 30 points the next day. But a month or two later most stocks were selling at lower prices.

"Whether it was the Eisenhower heart attack, the deaths of the two Kennedys, the Kennedy confrontation with the steel industry, the Cuban Missile Crisis, Johnson's decision not to run for re-election, the effect of the Vietnamese war which in the beginning was bullish, then later bearish, at some point, either over the short or the long term, the public goes too far. They both outdo and undo themselves. These are the times that markets can fall apart if a specialist loses his head and does what the rest of the mob is doing. These are the times I have to be most careful because I am human too. Whatever you are thinking, I too am thinking.

"People shouldn't buy or sell stocks when they are all hopped up about something. If they want to be successful they have to realize that the effect of whatever is causing them to act will usually disappear in a few days. Then, when they regain their senses they can make a more rational decision. Usually by waiting, investors will not only get a better price on their trade but they will get involved in fewer trades that produce losses.

"Investors sometimes think that we look forward to these emergencies; that we like to exploit them for our own benefit; but a person has to be either very naive or must have an extremely poor opinion of himself and others to think that anyone looks forward to disasters. We look forward to small tugs of war where investors alternately move stocks up, then down again. That's where we make our money. But we prefer not to see catastrophes because then everyone stands to lose.

"Don't think I'm crazy when I say this but I think weather sometimes has a lot to do with the market. I don't quite understand it, but when the weather is good and the air is clear the market often goes up, while when it's bad the market is often bearish.

"Maybe what happens is that when there is a bad storm somewhere, for instance, a lot of stockholders are more interested in digging their cars out or getting to work than they are in calling their brokers with orders to buy stock. There don't have to be many people in this position. Even a few people who don't get their buy orders in is enough to tip the scales down for the day.

"A successful specialist has to have the ability to recognize trends. He looks to see how people react to good news, to bad news or to no news at all. If investors do something other than what is obvious under the circumstances, this becomes extremely significant to the specialist.

"Many specialists don't bother but I watch money rates. I study changes in money rates to determine whether or not any changes are having their desired effect.

"I look to see the kind and quality of stocks investors are buying to determine the quality of the market. I look to see where volume is concentrated. I look to see if investors are trading stocks normally or if there is a concerted pattern of selling in certain stocks with a switching of proceeds into other categories. I look at which stocks people are ignoring as well as the ones they are rushing to buy.

"It is important for a specialist to know if activity in a stock is reasonable, logical and carefully measured or if it is irrational. I usually ignore the first 10 to 20 per cent of a stock's rise but then I carefully study its first reaction. If the stock doesn't react much; if the original buyers don't sell out; and, if new buyers come in, I know the stock is in the early stages of a new uptrend. To the extent possible, I attempt to position myself accordingly. On the other hand, if the original buyers sell and no new buyers come in, I know the stock was just being touted by someone for what they hoped would be a quick move. This is the kind of data that I consider important in my evaluation of a stock.

"Meetings with company officials? I never initiate any myself. Usually I avoid them except on a social basis with others present. Anything else is likely to be misconstrued by somebody, so who needs any more problems than they have?

"From a practical point of view, I find that if I pay attention to what the market is saying, it generally tells me more about a stock than any corporate officer possibly can. For instance, no company president is ever going to tell you that his company is on the verge of falling apart at the seams. That's not his job. His job at times like these is to sell confidence in the future to his staff, his suppliers, his customers and me. If he himself doesn't believe and can't sell that belief, he's not worth the money he's getting. Therefore, if anything, he will lead me astray.

"But this really is no big problem. There are much better ways to find out indirectly what is happening at a company. Ways that are readily available to me. For example, one of my neighbors is a vice president of a major textile company. They buy a lot of yarn from Spun Yarns, Inc., one of my stocks.

"I use him to keep me informed about Spun Yarns because anything he knows is probably open gossip in the trade. It's public information. When the company has a problem, he tells me. My neighbor tells it to me straight, like it is, not like it ought to be. Anything I get from him I can be confident about using, and, at the same time I don't have to worry about inside information. If he tells me something detrimental, I can be sure everyone in the trade already knows it. Of course, the market will already have told me that something is wrong. All my friend will do is tell me what it is.

"A specialist looks at the general news too. Things like strikes, for instance. I look to see how quickly a strike is settled or even if there is a strike. When people think times are bad, they are more interested in preserving what they have than in grabbing for more. Therefore, either they don't go on strike or they settle quickly. To me, when people are concerned about their economic well-being, they aren't going to be thinking about buying stocks no matter how good the value.

"I look to see if stocks are active because of big block activity or a large number of small tickets. If the volume is from small tickets, I look at the depth of the interest. Are the orders all coming from a few brokerage houses that always seem to buy and sell together or is the interest dispersed throughout the country?

"If I see widespread activity by the general public I try to find out whether someone is tipping the stock, or if people who are using the products of the company, for instance, are so impressed that they want to own the stock.

"A specialist learns to recognize what people are trying to do and notes how rationally they are going about their business. If I see someone trying to intelligently buy or sell a large amount of stock, I will do whatever I possibly can to assist him. If I can't help, at least I will not interfere with or frustrate his activities.

"On the other hand I let the irrational investor fend for himself. This is what brings on most criticism of specialists. The irrational investor not only hurts himself but he hurts others as well by the volatility he creates in a stock. Then, after he hurts himself, he complains because someone did not save him from himself. It's not that I do anything to violate the rules but it's like everything else in life. With some people you do what is required, while with others you go out of your way to help if you can.

"The person most interested in whether a stock sells high or low is the company president. Regardless of what anyone thinks I can't help him with the price level. That is up to him. If I do my job well his market will be orderly. If he does his job well people will want to own his stock and its price will go up. All he has to do is run a successful company, make a good product, earn a good rate of return, develop a motivated staff of employees and then tell the world about it. If he's done all the right things, people will rush to get on his team. If he hasn't, the crowd will find someone who has.

"One area where I disagree with the Wall Street pundits is in the ability (or lack of ability) of the odd lot customer. Unlike our counterparts at the New York Stock Exchange, we handle all our own odd lot business here. Over the years it has been my observation that the small investor is very perceptive about market matters and that it is worthwhile paying close attention to what he is doing.

"Although his impact on the market is small in terms of the amount of money he brings into the market, the odd lot investor represents the kind of decision making being done by the thinking, investing public as opposed to the more dilettante investor. The odd lot investor is generally someone who has not come by his money

easily. As a result he knows the value of it. He doesn't invest it reck-
lessly or foolishly. He buys only after long, deliberate analysis. Of all
investors in the market, I personally find a greater kinship with the
odd lotter than with any other investor group.

"The small investor is very good at market bottoms. When I see
him coming back into the market after a severe decline, my own
confidence that the decline is or soon will be over increases.

"When it comes to selling though I don't pay as much attention
to him as I do the individual who buys in 500 or 1,000 share lots.
These are the people who know when to sell. Every time the market
gets into a top zone, I get a rash of orders to sell from wire houses
all over the country in lots of 500 and 1,000 shares.

"At market tops, the odd lot investor is like the rest of us. His
thinking tends to get a little out of kilter as he gets caught up in
the hysteria of high prices and high volume. But though he lets his
guard down a little, he's nothing like the mutual fund boys playing
with other people's money and buying dozens of 50 and 100,000 share
blocks right at the top. At the top the small investor never loses sight
for long of what he's doing, because he's doing it with his own
money. The mutual fund boys with none of their own money at stake
don't have the same kind of motivation.

"If I had to summarize my operating philosophy, I would have to
say it's all a matter of judgement. I have better judgement when it
comes to the stock market than most people simply because I am
disciplined and concentrate my interests. That's why I consistently
make money. I am cool under fire. I make rational judgements
quickly. Few people have the ability to commit as much money so
quickly. Most do so only after weighing the consequences for hours,
perhaps days. Then they only invest after first convening a committee
to diffuse the blame if they should prove to be wrong. It's either
judgement or a superb instinct. It's not intelligence because I am not
significantly smarter than many others: Whatever it is, it works and
I am grateful for it."

14

Factors Affecting the Price of a Stock

SPECIALISTS ARE sometimes criticized by listed company officers for not sufficiently concerning themselves with the operations of their particular companies.

"Why doesn't he ever call on us?" is a frequently voiced complaint.

"He's not even on our mailing list and he doesn't seem to care at all about us," is another frequent but ludicrous comment in view of the fact that the company's mailing list is controlled not by the specialist but by the company itself.

"How can he possibly set a fair price for our stock when he's never visited us. I'll bet he doesn't know anything about us; what we make; what we earn; the condition of our plants; the quality of our sales force; the depth of our distribution network. He doesn't know any of these things. I could name you at least 50 analysts and brokers who know more about us than our specialist. These are people who are interested enough to call us once in a while and keep in touch. On the other hand, our specialist's indifference to us is a big source of annoyance and disappointment."

In commenting on observations such as this, Larry is quick to point out that he and his partners do indeed keep in very close touch with the operations of their companies but they do it indirectly through analysts, the company's competitors, trade journals and other sources. He is equally quick to say that he plays only a minor role in setting the price of his stocks. The investors who trade the stock play a much more important role. To them the operating outlook of any company is just one of the more important factors in the equation that determines the price they are willing to pay or accept. Because it is just one factor, often it is not even an important factor while at other times it may be exceedingly so.

Anybody who works with stocks as intimately as specialists, soon comes to realize that many different forces are at work in the market place. Some of these are tangible, visible and highly quantitative while others are intangible. Few investors have any idea of the numerous forces that interact on each other.

Obviously, if a company doubles its earnings over the previous year, this will have an effect, but sometimes the effect is not what one might expect it to be. For instance, if investors for one reason or another have come to expect that company earnings will triple they may be disappointed if earnings merely double. In their disappointment they might sell causing the stock in question to fall in price on the announcement of the earnings. The reason is not due to a poor performance on the part of the company but rather a disillusionment of investors that their fondest expectations did not materialize.

If Congress grants tax relief or imposes a new tax on business, this also has an effect. Again, strange as it may seem, sometimes it is the desired effect while at other times an opposite effect occurs. Whatever the standard, often the reaction is quite different than what was reasonably and logically expected.

Brokerage house recommendations have an effect. Institutional and insider market activity also have an effect. But again, sometimes they do not. Whether or not they do, other forces sometimes are more important.

For example, just being "tuned in" is important. If a person has never heard of a company, it might as well not exist as far as he is concerned. There is no way that he is going to help generate the pressure needed to push the price of the stock up regardless of how attractive the company's record might be. If the only interest a stock generates comes from holders looking to sell, their selling pressure will cause the price to drop. Therefore before anything positive can happen to a stock, people have to know about it. Once they know about it, then they have to want to buy and hold.

Thus, specialists tend to concern themselves with what people are actually doing at any particular time as opposed to what logic dictates they ought to be doing.

Larry claims his business forces him to react in the market on the assumption that most market orders are irrationally entered while most limit orders are logically initiated after a calm assessment of the situation. He recognizes that the person employing logic may often reach erroneous conclusions but at least he has given serious thought to what ought to be done.

He believes that when there is concentrated buying or selling by investors employing market orders, the investors are likely to be wrong. He recognizes that moods and attitudes of investors are variable, not constant. Therefore, he accords the constantly changing moods of investors a legitimate place in the equation of what determines the price of a stock.

To Larry, the tangible factors about a stock are only important when considered in conjunction with the intangibles. If an investor has heard of a company, the important thing to Larry is what does he think about it? Is he enthusiastic or does it leave him cold?

Perhaps the most important tangible factor is the earnings record. If a company has a consistent history of earnings increases and, if this favorable earnings history coincides with over-all bull market conditions, each dollar of earnings is likely to be valued at increasingly higher multiples. This may not always be true, but it seems to happen often enough to be valid.

Another factor in determining the direction of prices in recent years has been the increasing use of chart books and other technical considerations.

Still another factor is the volatility or speed with which a stock moves from one price level to another. This is often influenced by the float. Float is a term used to denote the number of shares of stock a company has outstanding free of legal restrictions making it immediately tradable. To be eligible for listing on Amex a company must have a float of at least 400,000 shares in the hands of the public. At the other extreme, a stock like American Telephone and Telegraph has a float of about 550 million shares.

Float is important in determining potential volatility because, generally speaking, the fewer shares of stock in the float, the more erratic will be a stock's price movements when concentrated buying or selling appears.

A small float might prevent some people from considering purchases. For example, mutual funds accustomed to purchasing stocks in quantities of 50,000 or 100,000 shares cannot, under most circumstances, buy into a stock with a 400,000 share float without bidding up the stock in such a manner as to create almost unbelievably chaotic pricing conditions in the stock. Then if they ever succeeded in acquiring such a block, they could hardly hope to sell without again disrupting the price pattern of the stock.

Volatility is also a function of the general level of activity in the stock. Few investors can effectively operate in a low float stock when volume is also low. Then, as trading interest increases, stocks with relatively small floats can accommodate larger numbers of investors.

Company managements have an important effect on the price of their stock in numerous ways. Their most important effect rests in their ability to make their companies profitable and well-respected in their industry. A company that manages to consistently achieve an above average return will often sell at a higher price than one which does not.

Management also affects the price of its stock by the image it projects. This image may be a reflection of competence or it may be entirely divorced from it. Image may be projected in many ways; by the style of the annual report for instance. A company concerned about its image will publish an attractive annual report complete with numerous pictures and items which may or may not be relevant but which nevertheless add readership interest to the reports.

A company oblivious to its public image on the other hand will include little more in its annual report than what is legally required of it. Not only this, but it often does so in the least atractive format imaginable.

A company's image is reflected in its advertising, its product packaging, the style and information content of its announcements, its social awareness and in other ways.

Also the image is reflected in the candidness and forthrightness of its management. Generally speaking, a management that is candid at all times will tend to command a higher price multiple and its stock will decline relatively less on unfavorable news than will the stock of a company that is not always so candid. This is especially true of a stock with a high price-earnings multiple. When such management loses the trust and the respect of its sponsors and investors, its decline from favor can be almost instantaneous.

The fact that a stock is or is not listed on an exchange can have an impact on a stock's price.

Some investors refuse to buy a stock unless it is listed on an exchange because they have greater confidence trading a stock whose price and volume data can be precisely followed. They like to know their trades are always executed at the best available price of the moment. They also like to know that market orders for reasonable quantities of stock will never be too far out of line with the lastest reported market price.

The other side of the coin is that exchanges sometimes lull an investor into a sense of complacency. Exchanges imply a degree of supervision into internal corporate affairs they are unable to deliver. Sometimes, too, an exchange's activities in policing its stocks result in bigger fluctuations to stocks than would otherwise occur.

Too, the exchanges are beginning to seriously view the corporate responsibility of timely disclosure. Thus, when the Amex learns that certain people are buying or selling on the basis of information not available to other investors, it demands that the company issue an announcement making the information available to all investors. Its reason is to see that no one segment of the market holds an unfair advantage in its trading over the other segments. This is great except that trading is increasingly being halted pending such disclosure announcemnts. The trading halts call attenion to the stock with the result that investors who might not otherwise think of trading the stock enter orders. This tends to accentuate existing pressures sometimes causing larger than normal price changes on the opening trade after the trading halt.

At other times to dampen excessive speculative pressures, exchanges will alter the normal rules of trading. One way is to announce that until further notice certain stocks can be traded, but only if the speculator puts up his cash in advance of the trade.

A special trading provision such as this in no way reflects on the integrity or the quality of the company. Instead, it is designed to highlight the fact that speculative interest in the stock is excessive for the amount of stock available for trading. This has caused the stock to become overly volatile and difficult to handle in a fair and orderly manner.

By putting stock on the 100 per cent margin list, the exchange is serving notice that it has become excessively risky for the average investor. For the time being, he should exercise extra care in entering orders. This restriction has the effect of eliminating from the market the most marginal investors who can least afford the high level of risk inherent in the stock at the time.

The quality of the specialist's performance also has an effect on the price of a stock because the better his performance relative to existing market conditions, the more confidence it will give people to trade the particular stock.

A good specialist will not become disoriented. He must also have the financial resources to cope with any pressures confronting a stock. Although their roles force them to be antagonists, he must also be able to do business with brokers in such a way as to hold their respect and confidence thus making them partners in keeping the market orderly.

Finally, there is the effect on the market of the Securities and Exchange Commission. The effect of the S.E.C. is most often indirect. When it is visible, it is most likely to appear negative because most items relating to the S.E.C. concern this agency's actions against those people who have violated securities laws.

By far its most important effect on stocks evolves from the laws it enforces to insure that investors get complete information from companies that are publicly traded.

Nevertheless, the action of the S.E.C. is beneficial. It requires companies to fully disclose what the S.E.C. considers to be significant corporate operating data. It cannot force an investor to use this information but it at least forces corporate officials to make the information available for those few investors who do care to use it. At the same time, under the threat of legal penalties, it insures that these reports have at least some basis in fact, however tenuous that may sometimes be.

15

Setting the Price on Opening Day

THE PRICE at which a stock trades is more or less automatically determined by the market forces of the moment except on two occasions: When a stock is reopened after a forced halt in trading, and on the opening trade of the day it is first listed. The opening trade is arbitrary because of the difficulty in gaining precise trading information on over-the-counter trading. Recently, this problem has been somewhat relieved as a result of the introduction of the over-the-counter automated quotation system called NASDAQ.

Whenever his unit is awarded a stock about to be listed, Larry arranges for someone in his clearing firm to trace the stock on NASDAQ. What he looks for are the number of market makers quoting the stock, the frequency with which quotations change, the average spread quoted by most of the dealers and both the "inside" and "outside" quotes. The "inside" quote is the best bid and offer being made in the stock, not necessarily by the same dealer, while the outside quote represents the widest spread being recorded.

The number of market makers tells Larry whether the stock has a broad market following or a concentrated one. It also indicates how active the stock is likely to be and tells something about its potential profitability. Because Larry knows that over-the-counter, no one is obliged to make a market in any stock unless he wants to, a large dealer following tells him that the stock not only is actively traded but potentially profitable. Otherwise it would not attract a large number of dealers competing for "a piece of the action." He then fine tunes his estimate of the market by studying the quotations being recorded. If he sees that the highest bid of one dealer is close to the lowest competing offer by another dealer he can assume that the stock will enjoy a reasonably active market; one in which he can take fairly large positions with relative safety when necessary.

A narrow outside spread tells him that all the interested market makers are actively and competitively quoting the stock while a wider spread would tell him that some of the dealers are more interested either in buying or selling than in providing active trading markets. All these things together give him a fair idea of the quality, depth and volume of trading activity that the stock is likely to enjoy.

Next, Larry looks at the volatility of the stock and its short-term price trend especially in the few days just prior to its listing. If the stock runs up rapidly just before listing to a degree that is out of proportion to the general market, he suspects that the run up may be engineered by someone trying to set him up to buy large amounts of the stock at inflated prices as soon as the stock gets listed.

On the other hand, a stock that is either trendless or moving only gradually probably represents fairly accurately that stock's current true market value.

By opening day, Larry has a good idea of approximately where the stock should open and what his tactical strategy for managing the stock should be. For instance, he might decide that based on its most recent O-T-C activity, the stock should open at about $15 barring any surprises immediately prior to the opening. Using this as his compass point, he adjusts the price either up or down depending on how many and what kind of orders come in for execution at the opening.

For starters, he knows that the president or someone else connected with the company is going to purchase the first 100 shares traded. If that is the extent of the activity or if the buy and sell orders equally offset each other, the specialist will open the stock at $15. If, however, there is a moderate imbalance of orders of perhaps 200 to 500 shares, he might open the stock slightly above or below $15 depending on whether buyers or sellers predominate. The larger the imbalance, the further away from $15 will be the opening price.

It is traditional but not mandatory for a company official to purchase the first 100 shares to kick off trading. This opening trade is not only traditional but is a practical necessity. Without it, it would be impossible to guarantee that a stock will begin trading on schedule. Under these circumstances, the only way for a trade to take place would be for the specialist to print a trade in which he is both the buyer and the seller. A trade of this kind is forbidden on two counts. First, a specialist is forbidden from engaging in wash sales. Second, he is precluded from initiating transactions merely to give the appearance of volume. With all the ceremony that revolves around the listing of a new stock, therefore, the order for the first 100 shares insures that trading actually will commence at the date and time designated.

Although the market itself opens for trading at 10:00 a.m. the official opening of a new listing is deferred until 11:30 a.m. This time lag gives the specialist an opportunity to direct his full attention to opening his other stocks, get the heavy first hour of trading out of the way and get a last minute reading on his new stock in the over-the-counter market.

Just prior to the opening, Larry will confer with a floor official to get approval for the intended opening price. The floor official reviews the condition of the book at the opening in relation to its most recent over-the-counter activity. When they mutually agree on a satisfactory opening price, the specialist opens trading. The official then signs the reporter's ticket of the first trade to certify that it was made with his approval.

The floor official usually explains to the corporate party the details surrounding the opening trade and precisely how the opening price was decided. Of course since all this is in the professional jargon of the Floor they probably don't have the faintest idea of what he is talking about. In any event, they are usually so excited at seeing the symbol for their stock flash across the ticker tape that they don't care. That is, unless the stock opens much below their expectations.

Promptly at 11:30 a.m., the opening trade is transmitted to the computer which drives the ticker tapes in brokerage offices all over the world. In just a few seconds the whole world will know that a new stock has opened for trading as something like the following rolls across the ticker:

AMEX WELCOMES POW . . . . OPENING TRADE 15¼ . . . .
1600 . . . . 15¼

This message tells the world that a new stock, with the ticker symbol POW has just been listed and its opening trade was on a total volume of 1,700 shares at 15¼. The first 100 shares represented the ceremonial 100 shares purchased by POW's president while the remaining 1,600 shares were traded by public customers.

In arriving at the opening price, the specialist took into consideration the following orders to buy and sell on his book:

Buy		Sell
500	Market	700
600	14	
100	⅜	
400	½	
700	¾	
700	⅞	
1,100	15	
500	⅛	
800	¼	200
400	⅜	
	½	1,000
	¾	500

To arrive at the opening price, he sees market orders to buy 500 and sell 700 shares. This means that the smallest opening possible would be a 700 share opening.

He could conceivably open the stock anywhere between 14 and 15¾ because he has orders both to buy and sell at various prices between these two extremes. As a practical matter, however, his discretion to act is much more severely limited.

If he wants to open the stock at 14, it would be necessary to open trading on 5,800 shares because with an opening at this price, everyone willing to pay more than 14 is entitled to buy at 14. This is the old story of supply and demand. If you are willing to pay $15 for an article someone is willing to sell for only $14, then you are entitled to make your purchase at $14 if that is all the seller is charging other buyers.

A $14 opening has two disadvantages. First, it does not represent the true level at which buyers and sellers are willing to trade directly with each other. This is evidenced by the fact that to open the stock at 14 requires the specialist going short 5,100 shares because he has orders from sellers for only 700 shares at this price. The fact is most buyers are willing to pay much more.

Then too, an opening at 14 would cause the stock to drop a full point from its most recent O-T-C bid.

At 15, the stock would have to open on 3,300 shares. An opening of this size would include orders to buy 500 shares at the market, 1,100 at 15, 500 at 15⅛, 800 at 15¼, and 400 at 15⅜. To handle an opening block of this size would have demanded that Larry go short 2,400 shares. This too is more than would be expected of him, especially in a new stock that he knows so little about.

On the other hand, opening the stock at 15¾ would clean up all the sell orders on his book. It would require him to open POW on a volume of 2,400 shares. At this price Larry would have to buy 1,900 POW shares and would cause the stock to move up ¾ point from its current O-T-C bid. Again, this is not satisfactory because it is not in line with the requirement that he trade as little as possible for his own account.

With the condition of the book as shown here the price that requires the least participation is 15¼. At this price the bid of 500 at market as well as the orders to buy 800 at 15¼ and 400 at 15⅜ are executed. Offsetting these are orders to sell 700 at market and 200 at 15¼. To complete the opening, he supplies 800 shares by going short. At 15¼ he fulfills his obligation to trade as little as possible while at the same time limiting the stock to a move of just ¼ point from its most recent O-T-C bid.

Setting this opening price is often an extremely risky proposition because specialists are not yet familiar with either the nature or size of the actual and potential interest in the stock. Neither do they know the manner in which this interest will manifest. Larry doesn't really know at what prices or quantities the stock has actually been trading over-the-counter. He knows the quotations, of course, but these are merely guides to the approximate range at which transactions are taking place. Unlike the exchange market where he has an obligation to provide price continuity, there is no similar parallel responsibility over-the-counter. As a result, it is possible for the level of quotes either to move up or down in the O-T-C market as a result of the competitive bidding practices of the dealers as much as from the competitive pressures of actual supply and demand. Furthermore, these competitive bidding practices can sometimes cause the market to move even when no actual transactions take place.

Within the limit of his discretionary power, Larry tries to open a stock as high as he can justify for the sake of the executive party from the company. He explains this by saying he doesn't believe there is one company president alive, who, despite his protestations to the contrary about not paying any attenion to the price of his stock, really doesn't want it to trade as high as possible. Therefore, Larry thinks it is good public relations on his part, to open the stock at it's maximum defensible level.

At the same time, however, he does not want to set the price so high that it attracts sellers immediately. He would like the stock to remain as stable as possible, perhaps even go up a little on the first day. What he hopes will not happen is to have the stock immediately take a dive. Some over-the-counter traders aware of this desire by most specialists to put their best foot forward for the company, try to dump stock onto the market immediately.

When asked about unusual openings, Larry remembers three that were of more than casual interest. One he especially remembers happened when no one in the corporate party wanted to place an order to buy stock at the opening.

"The company officials came down obviously in a party mood. I greeted them and asked their Exchange host if he knew the broker who was supposed to represent the company on the opening trade because no one had yet shown up with the order. The V.P. took me aside and whispered that the reason I had received no order was because no one in the company wanted to make the opening purchase.

"The company president said that he already owned over 40 per cent of the company and that he had absolutely no use for another 100 shares. In fact, what he was looking for was a broader market in order to sell his own stock as rapidly as possible. You can imagine the confidence an attitude like this gave me. We waited around for a few minutes for some public orders to come in but no one else was anxious to trade the stock either. I didn't know what to do, I felt I had an obligation to open the stock, all the rules about my not being allowed to initiate a trade notwithstanding. Finally, just before 11:30 Tommy, one of the few remaining floor traders walked by the post.

I took him aside, told him of my predicament and asked him to get me off the hook by entering an order. I didn't care whether he bought or sold. He agreed.

"With Tommy's order, I was able to open the stock. After the opening, the photographer came by to take the usual opening day publicity pictures. We chatted awhile, then went up to the conference room where the Exchange always throws a fabulous private luncheon for new listings. After lunch, I came back to the floor to find the stock still hadn't traded. Near the close, Tommy came back to cover his trade. The trade was an expensive one for me because I felt obligated to take Tommy and his wife out for a night on the town; dinner, show, cocktails afterwards, the whole works. It cost me a couple of hundred bucks but I felt it was worth it. Eventually there was some activity in the stock and it does reasonably well now. Much better, as a matter of fact, than I anticipated considering the circumstances of that initial meeting with the company.

"Another unusual opening occurred the time that a disgruntled O-T-C dealer decided to put pressure on a stock right on the opening trade. It's normal practice for some speculators to buy stock over-the-counter in anticipation of listing. History shows that stocks often run up in price during this period. Then, as soon as the stock is listed, these people turn around, sell and take their trading profits or losses. Most of us expect this sort of thing and adjust for it in our trading strategy. Actually, it's good that this occurs because with it, we are assured that someone is going to be there trading stock right from the beginning. This gives us the initial volume impetus we need.

"On this occasion, one O-T-C dealer deliberately did not work off his position prior to listing. Instead, he accumulated the stock in moderate quantities right up to the opening in order to keep the bid firm. Then, just before I was ready to open the stock, he came with an order to sell 6,500 shares at the opening. He deliberately intended to force me to drop my bid drastically. He wanted to embarrass me in the eyes of the company.

"I had been pretty happy about getting this stock. The company had a good track record and some fairly astute investors had spoken highly of the company. When it was announced that the company was applying for a listing, I made a special plea to get it. As usual, we followed the stock in the counter market. Because of this dealer the market stayed firm. It made us more and more confident that we had a potential winner in the stock.

"On opening day, I estimated that the stock should open somewhere between 16½ and 17. The first orders coming in were slightly biased toward the sell side but there was nothing especially unusual about this. All it meant was that there was just enough selling pressure to make me favor the lower rather than the upper end of my estimated opening range.

"The company came down about 15 minutes prior to the opening. This gave us a few minutes to become acquainted. During our conversation, I told them about my opening price intentions. While we were chatting, a broker came into the crowd with an order to sell 6,500 shares at the opening. Within the unit, Sammy was assigned the stock. I could see he was getting upset about something. I excused myself to see what the problem was.

"Heatedly he filled me in. He said he asked the broker to re-enter his order at a limit price. When he refused, Sammy asked him not to ruin the opening for the company but to come back later. The broker said he was aware of the effect his order would probably have on the opening. He said he too had questioned the order prior to bringing in to the post. He too had attempted to dissuade the seller. But he was given specific instructions that the order was to be entered at the market at the opening. According to the rules governing his conduct, he had to follow the instructions given him.

"This really played havoc with the opening. I was forbidden to discuss the matter with the company officials and it was too late for me to contact someone else who might be familiar with the company. I immediately got in touch with the listing representative who assisted the company with its listing application. He assured me there was no unusual corporate matters pending that he was aware of. Nevertheless, the order came from a broker who had an office in the city where the company was headquartered. This had me worried because it led me to the suspicion that the company was trying to pull a double cross of some kind.

"I was so furious that I lost my professionalism for just a moment. I felt like opening the stock at 10 but quickly snapped back. I knew an opening like that wouldn't sit well with anyone and in the days to follow, it would come back and haunt me more than once. By this time the floor governor supervising the opening arrived. After discussing the matter, we both agreed that under the circumstances, an opening at 13½ to 14 would be justified. But because this was the opening trade, he urged me to bend a little. He tried to persuade me to open the stock at 15. No way could he convince me of this. Finally he talked me into opening the stock at 14¾ on 7,300 shares of which I bought a whopping 6,900 shares.

"All this happened so fast that I didn't have a chance to say anything to the company. They knew that something was wrong but they weren't quite sure what the problem was either. In any event, when the company president saw his stock come across the ticker at 14¾, I thought he was going to go right through the roof and that is six floors above us. He became as incensed as I had previously been.

"It took a lot of talking but finally everyone calmed down. He said that an over-the-counter dealer had threatened to do just this if the stock were ever listed but he thought this was just an idle threat. The O-T-C dealer had been the company's original underwriter. From the time the company first went public, he had been its principal market maker. When the company first became eligible to list, the dealer, who found the stock extremely profitable, convinced the president that he should remain over-the-counter. He succeeded in holding on to the stock for several more years but the question of listing cropped up in discussions more and more frequently.

"Just as we don't like to lose one of our good stocks to the Big Board, this dealer did not want to lose his stock to us. This is a feeling I can well sympathize with. But at the same time, I was shocked at the vindictiveness of the dealer's actions when the company made its final irrevocable decision to list.

"Somewhere in their conversations, something happened to create a rift between the two men. The dealer apparently vowed to prove that the stock would never receive the kind of support he had given it. To prove his point he resorted to this scheme. He certainly succeeded in disrupting the opening. In addition he had another 3,500 shares in reserve which he used to dole out whenever the market was weak thus causing added pressure on the stock.

"This was embarrassing for a while but fortunately good buying developed a short time later. This helped support the stock near the opening price. As a matter of fact, in less than a year the stock doubled in volume that has been quite satisfactory. If anything, that dealer inadvertently did me a big favor by forcing me to take a bundle of stock at what turned out to be bargain basement prices.

"A third opening that stands out in my mind concerned a company managed by the type of people who consistently deliver a hard sell. On listing day, a small army of officers, press agents and others came to the Exchange to witness their opening.

"While the company officers were introducing themselves to their Exchange host, their public relations people asked to be excused to make a few last minute phone calls. They got in touch with the wire services with an announcement they wanted immediately released.

"Just as the corporate party set foot on the floor, all Hell broke loose around me. Brokers from everywhere began descending on me. Gene broke away from the post to contact the listing rep. He came running back with the news that the company had just announced that they intended to make a tender offer to buy a highly profitable company several times their size. Obviously this announcement was made with the intention of affecting the opening price.

"I called a floor governor to tell him that I had no intention of opening the stock until we found out just what kind of game these characters thought they were playing. This probably was the first time in history that trading was halted before it opened.

"The staff held an immediate meeting to get the whole thing cleared up. The riot act was read to the company. One of the things that bothered the Exchange in this case was the fact that the company disregarded a requirement to confer with the Exchange in advance of any significant announcement they planned to make. The staff knew the company couldn't plead ignorance on this one because their law firm was reputed to be one of the best in the business.

"While they didn't plead ignorance of the rules they tried to argue that they were exempt from Exchange regulations until the stock actually started trading. Since their announcement was made just prior to the initiation of trading they claimed exemption. To get an idea of their arrogance, they were threatening to sue the Exchange for the damage they said the delay was causing them. They knew this was not a defensible position but used it as a means of setting up a bargaining position from which to negotiate. The staff did not bite. They made it clear not only to the company but to the law firm as well that the rules applied to a company from the moment the Governors approved their listing application.

"A second and much more important concern to the staff was the fact that the company blatantly showed itself to be one that was going to try to actively influence the price of their stock. They were warned about the dangers and the problems activities of this sort might cause. To prove the seriousness of its intentions, the staff told the company that it's stock was immediately being placed under close Exchange surveillance. As one might expect, all this put a considerable damper on the merriment of the day.

"If we had opened the stock at 44, the O-T-C bid just prior to the announcement, we would have had to go short over 15,000 shares. Although it was evident from the crowd that developed that this was going to be an active trader, we all agreed never to voluntarily take big positions in this stock. Our decision meant that the stock might be more than usually volatile. But since we had been put on notice that we might otherwise be burned, this seemed to be the best business decision to make.

"It must seem like quite a switch to hear me talk about the reliability of a company. Usually it is our reliability that is questioned but these things can and do work both ways. As a result of our policy decision, we opened the stock at 49¾. At that price we went short just 1,300 shares. The floor governor working the opening gave me a lot of static about this price but I held firm. He finally relented.

"Although the company party tried to hide its enthusiasm, it was obvious they were delighted with the high opening price. Though the stock was to sell somewhat higher, the opening price turned out to have been well-chosen as subsequent market action proved. After opening at 49¾, it went to 50 before closing the day at 49½. It also closed as one of the 10 most active stocks which is a most unusual opening day performance.

"Subsequent events seemed to prove that all the chickens came home to roost concurrent with the listing of the stock. Within months a sell off began which did no cease until 5 years later. This shows what can happen when a company is too aggressive in touting their stock. They scare away the investment types leaving only traders who run at the first sign of trouble.

"Once the slide started, I heard through the grapevine that company officials were complaining about me. They remained critical of the delayed opening, saying that we had abdicated our responsibilities. They said the only reason we delayed the opening so long was so that we might short more stock. They claimed the reason I did not open the stock at 44 was that I wanted to short bundles of it at 49¾. No way was that true. Had I allowed the stock to open at 44 and then let the stock run up to 49¾ on the immediate excitement generated by their news, we might have ended up short 25,000 or more shares instead of the 1,300 we actually shorted. In view of the subsequent price action by the way, this would not have been a bad move for us. By opening at 49¾, I participated less in the stock than I would have at any other level.

"Management also accused us of causing the stock's volatility, conveniently forgetting it was their own news announcement, timed as it was, that created the trading personality which the stock never lost. But then, being a specialist, it's easy to get people to believe the worst about you."

16

Learning to Handle a New Listing

THE THREE to six month period immediately following the initial listing of a stock is usually the most difficult period in a specialist's relationship with that stock. This is the "seasoning" period during which the stock develops its personality as it were. It is in this period that the stock develops the investor following and trading characteristics likely to stay with it for long time to come.

This is especially true if the first impression the public gets is one of volatility, coupled with abnormally high volume, or if the stock for some reason possesses a glamour or charisma that attracts investors or traders in large numbers. On the other hand, stocks that start out less spectacularly are likely to remain quiet for a long time. Many stocks start off quietly only to evolve into active traders. But unless a stock is struck with instant recognition a broad investor following might be difficult to come by. During this seasoning period the stock is likely to be only marginally profitable.

Actually a stock goes through several seasoning periods on its path to maturity. A stock trading on the New York Stock Exchange is likely to have experienced four or more seasoning periods before finally settling down into a dependable market pattern.

The first generally occurs when a new company first sells stock to outsiders. At this time, its public shareholders are likely to be under-writers and their close friends or people who are acquainted with and friendly to the original founders of the company.

Several years later, if the company continues to grow, it probably reaches a point where it is growing faster than it can generate funds internally. Or, possibly, some of the original shareholders may want to bail out their stock to the public by means of a public underwriting. There are recurring periods when stocks are fully priced. The com-pany is likely to select one of these periods to offer its stock.

The majority of buyers of such new issues turn their stock over within three to six months. Many of the people who follow are also looking for a quick trading profit but someone, at some point, for some reason decides to hold the stock for more than a few months. For whatever reason, a company's shareholder list eventually stabilizes and so does the trading pattern in the stock. If the company continues to prosper, it will reach a point where it meets the qualifications for listing on Amex. The company will weigh the advantages and disad-vantages as it sees them and arrive at a decision. Since most company presidents look forward to the day when their stock is trading on a national exchange, it often doesn't take much to convince them to seek a listing.

When the stock gets to the Amex it goes through another season-ing period. During this period the company gains a potentially large following of stockholders who choose to trade on exchange markets. At the same time they might lose their O-T-C following. In return for losing a variable dealer support, it gains a specialist supervised cen-tral arena in which to trade.

If investor interest is quick to focus on a newly listed stock and general market conditions are favorable, the seasoning period for a new stock can be quite brief. On the other hand, if trading interest lags with the O-T-C investors selling out long before new buying in-terest develops, the seasoning period can be agonizing especially so because precise trading data is so readily available to investors.

If the Amex seasoning period is difficult, the company president is likely to receive phone calls from complaining investors. They will urge the president to transfer to the Big Board at the earliest opportunity. Eventually, enough additional shares are distributed to qualify the stock for Big Board listing. Again an appraisal is made and again the decision might favor a transfer.

The recurring need to re-season an issue ends with a move to the Big Board and only then can a company arrive at a rational decision as to which market can best serve its interests and those of its shareholders. It does not automatically follow that each progressively higher step will improve a stock's marketability. There are times when every stock is difficult to trade. At such times the market maker, though he may be an O-T-C dealer or an exchange specialist is likely to be the subject of harsh criticism. There are other stocks that are always difficult to handle regardless of market conditions while a few would have a good market whenever they trade. Consequently, the investor/trader dynamics of some stocks are such that an intermediate market serves it better than the highest market for which it qualifies. There are times that an Amex pre-listing review indicates that although a company meets Amex lising standards its best market is likely to be over-the-counter. The Exchange may point this out to a company. It is difficult for a management to accept this judgement, however, because it appears to be an adverse reflection of their stewardship. At other times an Exchange analysis will indicate that a continued Amex listing will serve a company better than a transfer to the Big Board. But because this appears to be so patently self-serving, the opinion if advanced to a company often goes unheeded.

Therefore, the final seasoning on the Big Board is sometimes a most brutal affair. For whatever reason, larger blocks of stock sometimes come on the market in more concentrated fashion following a Big Board listing than after an Amex listing.

It is only when a stock becomes listed on the Big Board and its market is still lacking something that a company president finally realizes, though he may not care to admit it, that there is something about his stock and not the arena where it is traded that determines how good the market will be. A friend whose company once was listed on the Amex but is now on the N.YS.E. observed:

"Even after all your efforts to explain the market to me, I still don't understand it. When I was on Amex, people were continually complaining of the bad specialist we had. They convinced me we should transfer to New York. Now that we have made the change these people are still complaining, still cursing, still calling my current specialist the same names they called my Amex specialist. I don't know whether the people calling me know what they are talking about or not. I don't know whether my specialist is honest or not, whether he is good, bad or average and I don't care. I know I am going to get complaints no matter where my stock trades. At least now I can point to my Big Board listing and show everyone we have arrived."

Something similar was reported some time ago in the *Wall Street Journal* when that paper reported a conversation with a company officer who from time to time had been critical of the market when his stock was on the Amex. Now it was on the N.Y.S.E. and on the particular day in question the officer was bothered by his stock's volatility. Actually, he was annoyed by the fact that the stock went down. He told the reporter, "Basically it indicates to me that the specialist isn't doing his job. I saw the stock go down over three points recently on small volume and that shouldn't happen."

The reporter contacted the specialist for his comments. To his credit, this specialist fielded the question quite well. He asked the reporter to see if the company president was equally distressed with his (the specialist's) performance several days earlier when this same stock went up over seven points on equally small volume. The specialist correctly pointed out that he is judged by the continuity of pricing he provides for his stocks, and, in his opinion, a review of the continuity in this particular stock would show it to have been excellent both as it was moving up and down.

For anyone not intimately involved with these things, it is hard to imagine how irrationally some company officials will react to a difficult seasoning period. I recall once trying to get an appointment with a company president shortly after his company first listed.

When I called he was adamant in refusing to see me saying he didn't ever want to see anyone from the exchange again. He considered his market experience since listing a disaster because the price of his stock had dropped sharply. He strongly suggested that rather than traveling around the country consoling company presidents on their losses, the exchange do everything possible to help the specialist "jack the prices of all the stocks back up to where they belonged."

I later learned that the only reason this man listed his company was because he was eager to sell his stock via a secondary offering. He believed he could get more for his stock if it were listed than he could

O-T-C. But he waited too long and by the time the offering cleared the S.E.C. both the general market and his company's operations were trending down causing the price of his stock to drop. Actually, the price drop was rather mild considering the poor operating statements released by the company. But, to the officer to whom every point meant a loss of several thousand dollars this seemed like a disaster.

Those readers who want to review a specialist's personal trading activities in some detail are urged at this time to turn to appendixes C and D on pp. 179–182. Both schedules detail the specialist's purchases and sales of a new stock from the opening trade through the first three months of listing. The stock was initially listed about the time the general market made an intermediate peak. Subsequently a decline ensued which was reflected in the price of the stock.

Appendix C lists by price level all purchases and sales by the specialist for his personal trading account. Appendix D journalizes all his round lot purchases and sales in chronological order on a FIFO (First In-First Out) basis. Each price represents the purchase or sale of 100 shares. If the specialist purchased 300 shares of this issue at 21 for example, the number 21 is posted on the schedule three times. Chronologically, each sale is matched off against a purchase, the profit or loss on the round trip is computed and then shown on a cumulative basis.

17

The Specialist-Company Relationship

As a rule Larry has very little contact with officers of the companies whose stocks he trades. Unless he happens to be on vacation or on other business in the immediate vicinity of one of his companies, he doesn't visit them, he doesn't call them, he doesn't write them. It's not that he's unsociable. And it's not that he is arbitrary because any time an officer from one of his companies is in New York and drops by the Exchange, he is always a most courteous host.

"The problem I have with company officials is that the few who work hardest at trying to see me are the same people who sometimes seem most anxious to use me. They seem to delight in trying to leak all sorts of information we are not supposed to know. Then, at some point, they think they have the right to tell me how to manage their stock. If it were that easy we'd never lose money in our trading accounts. Sometimes I'd like to trade places with one of those guys for a month. If they did with their money what they want me to do with mine, they'd be broke in a month.

"I had one fellow tell me once that it would be a good idea if his stock went up 4 or 5 points because he was in merger negotiations. A

111

higher stock price would have meant that he would have to give away fewer shares in the deal. Someone else once wanted his stock lower for some crazy reason. For him, the lower the stock dropped, the better. Whenever someone approaches you in this manner, there is always trouble afterward. The problem is you don't know in advance what a fellow is going to say and you can't be rude by refusing to see him. What these people either don't want or care to realize is that if I am to survive, I cannot take orders from anyone but the market place itself. That is the only way to play this game."

On the Exchange floor, there are two schools of thought among specialists as to what the proper specialist-company relationship should be. Some successful, honest specialists will agree with Larry that they do their best work being isolated from all contact with the company. A few even go so far as to ignore analysts, company reports, and information of any kind. They prefer to work entirely with supply and demand in a vacuum from all other factors.

Another equally competent, group of specialists will argue just as strongly that they can serve the market best if they know everything that can be known about the company and the forces acting on the stock. They always qualify this by saying that they want no information not available to anyone outside the company, but once the information becomes public, they want to know about it as quickly as anyone else.

They argue that they can best serve the needs of stockholders only if they know everything about a company and its stockholders that a person can possibly know.

To a specialist who thinks this way, whenever a company invites analysts to visit their facilities, these specialists also want to be invited or to send along an analyst from their firm. When the company holds its annual meeting, the specialist will try to attend or send someone else in his place. He will buy the company's products or use its services to see how good they are. He will dissect their annual reports to get an idea of how conservative the company's accounting practices may be. He will try to meet every decision-making officer of the company to see how competent (or incompetent) they are. He wants to know how much of what the company announces in their press releases is likely to be froth and how much is solid substance. He wants to know everything he can to make a good market for his stock.

"Not so," says Larry and others who believe that everything a specialist needs to know can be learned from the orders entered at the post. "You have to expect that with a vested interest in the future behavior of a stock, they will color the facts they release, but the pattern that orders trace in the market never lie except to the person who insists on closing his eyes to what he sees. If a company is running into serious start-up problems in a new plant that was supposed to revolutionize the industry, do you think the president is going to tell me about it? You're damn right he won't. At best, he will tell me they have the usual start-up problems you can expect at any new plant but otherwise everything else is coming along fine.

"Now, if I watch his stock's market action instead, I'll soon know that something is wrong because his suppliers and the people who work at the plant will know something is wrong. They may not sell stock themselves but they'll tell their friends about it. Soon I'll start seeing an increasing volume of orders to sell from brokers located in the vicinity of the new plant. If I pay attention to what the market is saying, I can alert Exchange officials to a possible problem. We might thus uncover something before too many potential buyers get hurt.

"But if I listen to the president, I might be tempted to support the stock unduly. I might be tempted to provide too much depth at higher prices. Then, when the company officially admits they are in trouble, I will have ended up helping no one except the people who sold out earlier. The price of the stock will collapse on the announcement instead of having fallen gradually. I'll lose a bundle on the stock. I won't have the money to support the stock properly when the really heavy selling comes in and I won't have allowed the stock to signal its warning ahead of the news to those few investors who, like me, are usually discerning enough to pick up these hints by the action of the stock."

The Amex has been silent on this as a matter of official policy. Officially, it neither forbids nor encourages this kind of communication. The rules merely say that neither specialist nor company officials are permitted, in any discussions they might have with anyone, to divulge information that is confidential or what would be considered to be inside information.

Under these requirements, the company is not permitted to tell the specialist anything that has not been released publicly prior to their discussions. On the other hand, the specialist is legally prohibited from divulging to the company the size of his book in their stock, the price levels at which open orders are entered, the names of brokers active in the market or anything of a similar nature. In other words, meetings between company and specialist are not specifically prohibited, but it is expected that any such meetings will be between two honorable parties, neither of whom will, by reason of the confidential nature to which both are privy, take advantage of their position.

The basis of a specialist's reluctance to enter into a close relationship with officers of companies they represent goes back to the early 1960s. At that time an improper relationship between two specialists and a company president enabled the company to illegally sell unregistered stock to investors. The specialists involved were imprisoned and for a while there was serious doubt that the Amex would stay in business. The controls on specialist performance discussed in this book are a direct result of these scandals. They are a tribute to the good end results that often come of adversity. Company presidents foolish enough to list during those days sometimes reminisce with laughter at the extremely circumspect manner in which the reforming administration conducted themselves.

They speak of the marvelous treatment they received at the hands of the staff, the thrill of seeing that first sale go over the ticker tape and the luncheon that followed. How they remember that luncheon! They still smile at the lecture they received at the conclusion of the lunch by Ed Posner, the first chairman of the reorganized Exchange.

"Gentlemen," he would begin, looking first into the eyes of the specialist and then the company president. "You have met each other. You both know that the other is a warm human being and not a faceless monster. You both know that the other is an honorable man who will do his best for you under all circumstances. After this meeting, I want you (looking at the specialist) to go back downstairs and give this stock the best market that you are capable of and I want you (looking at the company president) to go back to your company and run it as profitably as it is in your power to run it. One final thing. I don't want either of you, under any circumstance, ever to meet each other again. You don't need to get together because each of your jobs are mutually exclusive of the other."

This, of course, was an overreaction to what had preceded but under the circumstances, it undoubtedly appeared justified, since then the Amex has cautiously moved in the direction of re-opening lines of communication.

Nevertheless, Larry still prefers to keep his contacts with listed companies as minimal as possible. "You ask me, Why? I'll tell you why." He says: "A couple of years ago I went to the wedding of a daughter of a distant cousin. At the wedding, I'm sitting next to this guy and it turns out that he's with the S.E.C. We got to talking and I tell him the names of some of the companies I specialize in. I came to one name and he made a terrible face. I pumped him on his reaction and it turns out that at the S.E.C., the man who runs the company is considered to be real bad news.

"I remember several years back he was making a lot of static because I had refused to see him. He was trying to force a meeting with me through the staff. I never told anyone the reason for my refusal at the time. But in the late 1950s and early 1960s when they were picking off all those people like Alexander Guterma, Tony Di Angelis, Earl Bell and Louis Wolfson for various kinds of securities swindles, it turned out that our friend was supposed to have approached one of the men convicted during that era. He was supposed to have masterminded one of the swindles. Then, when the heat was on, he became a prosecution witness and blamed the whole thing on the man that was sent to jail. I'm not saying the story is true because I don't know the facts. All I know is the company he now heads is certainly a good one. Its growth record is impressive. It trades well for us. It makes money for me and for a lot of the people who trade the stock from time to time. The man seems honest and respectable. He is certainly very capable.

"Nevertheless, I do not want to chance seeing him. I've got too much to lose. If I didn't know about his alleged past, things might be different. I don't mind it when the president of one of my companies from out West (to a New Yorker that is anything beyond Jersey City) stops by with his wife and kids when they're in town on their way to Europe or something like that. They don't know so much about my business that I have to worry about a slip of the tongue coming back years later to haunt me. When I talk to them about the market, they probably don't know what I am talking about anyway. But I do have to be much more discreet talking to someone who knows more about the market than some of the younger members here on the Floor."

As Larry's comments indicate, the problem of current company-specialist relationships is an extremely difficult and sensitive one. Where men of integrity are concerned, the prohibitions against all contact between these two very important men is unduly harsh. On the other hand if either the specialist or the company president were to display the frailties characteristic of so many humans, the damage they could create is incalculable.

Fortunately, most men on both sides of the fence use more than a normal amount of caution and discretion in their relationships with each other. Most make it a point not to come in contact with each other except in public situations with others present.

Company presidents too recognize the advantages of a wholesome relationship and the dangers of a relationship that is too close. Like Larry, most do not want to become so close that the relationship might develop dangerous overtones. In the words of one company president:

> "All I want to do is meet the specialist every year or two so that I know who he is and he knows who I am. I want to feel I can trust him and have confidence in him, knowing that he is doing the best for my stock that he can. At the same time, I want him to know me so he can believe I am doing the best job possible for my company. That way, when that bear market comes around every few years and he gets hit with a lot of selling, maybe he'll be willing to pay an extra eighth of a point for my stock once in a while. And maybe he won't be so concerned when he has to hold our stock during times like those because he knows that we are competent to resolve our problems."

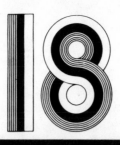

The Economics of Specializing

LOOSEN A specialist's tongue with a few drinks, then ask him how well he's doing. Odds are he will bore you stiff with a nonstop commentary of either all the big winners or the big losers he has masterminded during his career. By the time he's finished you'll wish you had never asked. But try to pin him down to a specific figure and he will become either extremely evasive, will clam up entirely or switch to another subject.

For a long time I felt that this evasiveness was due to a desire to hide from everyone how fantastically profitable the business of specializing is. With the passage of time and a bit of exposure to specialists, however, hints began to appear that perhaps being a specialist is not nearly as profitable as it is cracked up to be. Consequently, it appeared to me that the unwillingness to discuss earnings on the part of the specialist fraternity might be due to embarrassment on their part. They just don't want to admit to anyone, perhaps not even themselves, that they are not doing as well as everyone says they are.

Because of this reluctance to discuss earnings figures, it has never been possible to zero in precisely on how much money a specialist earns. So, we will have to do it more obliquely. One way is to look at life-styles. There is one specialist who takes extreme pride in owning two yachts that any mid-eastern potentate would be proud to own. He keeps one docked down at Ft. Lauderdale and uses the other as a jitney to shuttle himself and friends back and forth along the Intercoastal Waterway. On the other hand there are a half dozen specialists who make do with Volkswagens and Toyota's as their family cars. Getting down to something even more basic, there are always more specialists at lunch dining at the Exchange coffee shop or the workingman's bar across the street where a man-sized corned beef sandwich and glass of beer can be had for well under two dollars than in the posh exchange dining rooms where lunches go for three to five times that amount. One reason is time. You can get in and out of a coffee shop in 15 to 30 minutes which is about all the time that specialists can afford to take out of their day. But maybe money sometimes plays a part too.

During the euphoria of 1968 when daily volume on the Exchange sometimes reached 10 million shares, many young specialists with little real experience were bragging to their friends of earning $40,000. Actually earnings in the neighborhood of $60,000 to $75,000 were fairly common for a neophyte. In those years even clerks earned $15,000 to $20,000. A friend told my wife of her nephew, 19 years old who earned $21,000 in 1968 in his first job out of high school as a clerk on the Floor of the Exchange. He used to impress dates by flying the airline shuttle to Boston to dine at Loch Ober's seafood restaurant and flying back the same night. A year and a half later he was out of a job.

Unfortunately bull markets don't last forever and earnings of his magnitude didn't last long. On the heels of 1968 came 1969 and 1970, when losses instead of profits were the order of the day. The losses in a few cases were so big that some specialists like many nonprofessional investors not only gave the market back all their bull market profits but their own savings and, in some cases, the savings of their families as well. In 1969 and 1970, one rumor had it that the average specialist income was only about $20,000 or $25,000 and most specialists were grateful to have earned that. One source stated that some specialist clerks, since they were salaried, earned more than their employers in 1970.

But profit and loss figures, whether for a fixed period of time or for a hypothetical average specialist are deceptive. Regularly specialist units dissolve because a partner throws in the towel. He does not have the stamina or the money to outlast an adverse market. At the same time for those specialists who can hold out, sometimes the ones with the largest interim losses in a decline turn out to be the biggest winners in the advance.

This is supposed to be true of the specialist unit rumored to have the biggest trading losses in the bear market of 1969–1970. When the market turned around, demand for several of its stocks was so great that the unit not only recovered its bear market losses but made an unusually handsome profit as well. This only proves that the best way to judge the profitability of specializing is not to look at a fixed period of time but to cover an expanded time frame from the trough of one bear market to the trough of the next bear market. Otherwise some distorted ideas of profitability might arise. Thus, assuming that the average specialist income per man before taxes in 1968 was $100,000, if in the following 2 years he earned the rumored average of $25,000 per year, his total income for the 3 years was $150,000 or $50,000 on average. Not bad you might say but still not the high six figure income which one writer has stated they are "generally assumed to earn," nor is it as assured as critics outside the industry infer.

Getting back to 1970, most specialists were grateful to have earned anything that year because the April–May decline alone which dropped the Dow Jones Industrial Average from 800 to 630 caused most specialists to take the worst losses most of them have ever experienced. As a group, specialists lost an aggregate of about $5 million during the second quarter of 1970 before expenses. After expenses the figure was another million higher. In addition to their losses, every unit was carrying thousands of shares of excess inventory. The losses averaged out to about $35,000 or $40,000 per man. How would you like to go to work every day for three months only to have your pay check docked $35,000 at the end of that time?

Larry recalls vividly the day he received his May, 1970 operating statement. He was ecstatic because his unit had lost only $11,000 that month. Compared to what was happening to some units around him, he couldn't have been happier if he had made a million dollars. After seeing one of his friends forced into bankruptcy and others licking their wounds after taking huge losses, a mere $11,000 loss to him seemed as good as a profit. And indeed it was.

A breakdown of this loss is most interesting because it is so inconsistent with what one might expect. It also illustrates to the amateur the importance of letting a profit run because one big profit can wipe out dozens of mistakes. Of the 40-odd stocks in the unit, there were 29 in which they lost money. In these 29 stocks they lost a total of $58,000. This was offset by a $47,000 profit in the remaining 11 stocks. However, $35,000 of the profit came from just one stock while the remaining $12,000 was more or less equally divided among the remaining 10 stocks.

Unfortunately, other equally competent units did not fare nearly as well. On the morning of May 27, just as the market was getting ready to climax in preparation for beginning the new bull market, the bankrolling partner of one unit decided he had enough. He was a multiyear veteran who concluded that the 1970 market was worse than anything that had ever happened before and that it was going to get much worse before it got better. He could neither stand the heat nor the losses any longer. Without any advance notice to his partners, he pulled out of the unit. His partners came to work that morning to find their partner had virtually thrown them into bankruptcy. The panic button was pressed. A shotgun marriage was arranged and another crisis was avoided.

If this proves nothing else, it proves that specialists are not omniscient. It proves that even veteran specialists do not know any better than the rest of us what the market is going to do next. This veteran could not even foresee that a rally was just a few hours away. Like any odd-lotter, he sold out right at the bottom.

The successful specialist then is not an analyst nor is he an investor. Instead he is a merchant who knows the going value of his merchandise and does not attempt to correlate it to a theoretical value. He knows how to balance off the unequal forces of supply and demand at any particular moment.

Therefore, while I cannot tell specifically how profitable specializing is, there are some general observations that can be made which will hold true.

First, a specialist has no way of knowing which of his stocks is going to prove profitable. His biggest money maker one year is likely to be a millstone around his neck the next year.

Stocks which rationally "should" perform often fail to live up to their expectations. A few years back, for instance, a Canadian mining issue was approved for listing. Advance data showed the company had about 5,000 or 6,000 U.S. shareholders. It was reasonable to assume from this that the stock was going to be an active trader. The anticipated trading interest however, failed to develop, giving the assigned specialist one of the dullest issues in his portfolio. So dull in fact that many weeks the stocks does not trade.

One myth about specializing is that it is consistently profitable, that the specialist always makes his eighth of a point on every share he handles. This is not true. In fact, on balance, Amex specialists lost money in their trading accounts in 1969 and 1970 and in four of the eight quarters in 1971 and 1972. Sometimes trading losses are extraordinarily huge. There are no consistently profitable specialist units nor are there any consistently profitable or reliable stocks. When volume picks up and prices are rising so that the average investor is holding his own or making money, the specialist is also making money. But when the average investor is confused about the market, this confusion translates into a difficult climate for profitable specialist operations.

Specialists need activity in order to make money. As a rule of thumb, some say they need consistent volume of at least 2,000 shares per day, day in and day out in the average stock in order to give it a good market and at the same time have it profitable for themselves. Low volume in a stock generates complaints from investors because they cannot get what they consider good executions. At the same time it is difficult for the specialists because their fixed expenses continue with lower volume against which to offset these expenses.

The number of stocks assigned to a specialist unit has an important bearing on the potential profitability of the unit.

Statistically, if a unit has a dozen stocks or less, the probabilities are a unit will lose money on balance about one quarter every two years. On the other hand, as a unit gets bigger and as the number of stocks assigned to it increases, the probability of losing money decreases. A large unit, therefore, except for years like 1969 and 1970 when all the odds are thrown out the window, should benefit by the increased diversification of its portfolio.

Although his operations were profitable on balance, Larry expects to lose money in about half his stocks each year. He lost money in 16 of 39 stocks in highly profitable 1968, 27 of 41 in 1969, 23 of 44 in 1970, 20 of 48 in 1971 and 23 of 51 stocks in 1972.

Specialists tend to lose money whenever a stock either goes straight up or down in price. The reason of course lies in the fact that the steepness of a move is indicative of either a concentration of buying coupled with an absence of selling or conversely, of overwhelming selling pressure at a time when willing buyers are nowhere to be found. The specialist finds himself either buying or selling short abnormally large quantities of stock at average prices much less favorable than those at which he can close out his transactions.

For instance, assume that a stock has moved quickly from 10 to 20. By the end of this move the specialist might have a short position of 10,000 shares in the stock. He probably acquired this short position at an average price of $15 or $16. Then a reaction sets in during which time the stock reacts down to about $15. Even though the specialist manages to cover his short position during this reaction, it is unlikely that he will be able to do so at his average selling price. He will be most fortunate if he can cover at an average cost of $17 per share or a loss of as much as $10,000 on the round trip.

Then if the stock should move on its second leg of advance from $15 to $30 and if the specialist again goes short, he will suffer another loss when he covers. For this reason, volatile and unexpected moves are just as disturbing to most specialists as they are to most investors.

Another way to illustrate why many specialist transactions are unprofitable is to show what happens during a typical trading sequence where a stock first runs up, then down to the original trading level. In cases like this all the transactions net out at no profit except for the specialist's high sale and low purchase. For instance, if a specialist first bought 400 shares on successive down ticks at 40, 37⅞, 39¾, and 39⅝ then turned around and successively sold 400 shares at 39¾, 37⅞, 40 and 40⅛, his only profit would come from the purchase of 100 shares at 39⅝ which he then sold at 40⅛. The other trades at 39¾, 37⅞ and 40 would wash each other out. Therefore, a specialist's over-all profitability is determined by his ability to buy more stock in the low areas of trading ranges than he sells and to sell more at the top than he buys.

To get a detailed idea of the economics of specializing, we are going to review in detail specialist activity in the stock of Klunky, Inc. for a typical four-week period.

Klunky is an active stock; one that sometimes makes the most active stock list. It is a stock that is highly regarded by the unit handling it. The month reviewed is an average month which saw no disproportional price swings in either direction.

During the month, Klunky opened at 33 and closed at 32¼. In the interim, it sold as high as 36⅝ and as low as 30¾. Reported round lot volume during the month totaled 301,700 shares. General market conditions were average. Most market-wide indexes were down a few pennies during the month.

Of the 301,700 shares traded, the specialist participated as a principal, in round lot trades totaling 109,900 shares.

Of the remaining 191,800 shares the buyers of Klunky stock purchased their shares directly from sellers through broker intermediaries. Assuming that the specialist bought and sold an equal number of shares, he participated in about 18 per cent of all purchases and 18 per cent of all sales or 36 per cent of the total transactions. This is slightly above average but not enough above average to be especially significant. Therefore, the results of this study should be about as representative of what happens with a healthy active stock as it is possible to find. This stock was randomly selected with no advance indication of the profit contribution to the unit handling the stock.

Of the approximately 192,000 shares traded without the direct intervention of the specialist, brokers probably left limit price orders with the specialist either to buy or to sell stock on one side of the trade of 145,000 shares while the remaining 47,000 shares probably represented crosses, where a broker came to the specialist with orders both to buy and sell an equal number of shares.

Insofar as the 47,000 crossed shares are involved, the specialist received no compensation of any kind. His services here consisted merely of agreeing to report and print the transaction on the tape at the prearranged price. He received a commission on the 145,000 shares he held on his book for buyers and sellers at limit prices while on the remaining 109,900 shares that he traded for his own account, he was given the opportunity to make or lose money for his firm.

Every time a specialist accepts a limit price order from a broker, he receives a commission if and when that limit order is executed. On such limit orders, the specialist performs nothing more than a clerical function in that he holds the order for the broker and guarantees to execute the order if and when the limit price is reached. For performing this service the specialist is paid a floor rate commission by the broker.

This floor rate commission varies from a minimum of 25 cents to a maximum of $3.80 per 100 shares on stocks selling over $50 per share. The floor rate for a stock in Klunky's price range might average out to about $2.80 per 100 shares. Therefore, for supervising the execution of limit orders left with him in Klunky, the specialist received about $2.80 per 100 shares on the 1,450 round lots left with him or an estimated gross income of $4,060 for the month.

A stock like Klunky which not only trades in high volume but which sees numerous limit orders left with the specialist is called a ticket writer. Given a choice, most specialists would want every one of their stocks to evolve to the stage where they could be classified as ticket writers because such stocks represent good, clean income producers which can be merchandised at relatively little risk.

Trading profits provide the second source of income generated by the unit. Here, however, the income is potential rather than assured because of the possibility of loss as well as profit. In performing his dealer function a specialist acts involuntarily much of the time to moderate a stock's natural volatility. He must act as a stock's buyer or seller of last resort when others willing to perform that function are not available.

The dealer function caused the Klunky specialist to either buy or sell 109,900 round lot shares of stock during the month. Since there are no odd lot dealers on the Amex, specialists also function as odd lot dealers. In this capacity he purchased 8,773 shares in odd lots while selling 4,857 shares. Because of all this the specialist started out with a short position of 1,419 shares and ended long 3,416 shares. In between, he was long as much as 7,000 shares.

Since investors generally compute their profits and losses on a first in-first out basis, we will use that method in our illustration. On this basis, the specialist earned, $4,060 for handling the limit orders on his book, $6,077 on lot sales which he offset against odd lots purchased and $4,626.75 from his round lot trading activities. This gave him a total gross profit of $14,763.75. Appendixes E, F and G on pages 183–185 will show the round and odd lot transactions made at each price level along with a summary of how the above figures were arrived at.

Illustrative of earlier discussions, this $14,763.75 gross profit does not accurately reflect the profit in Klunky because if the specialist were to close out his month end inventory at that month's closing price, he would have suffered a loss of $9,467.25. The reason for this is because the stock closed the month at $32.25 while his inventory was purchased at an average per share price of $35.02.

Perhaps the table on page 125 will illustrate all this more clearly.

Whether or not this potential loss to the specialist materialized, we do not know, but that is relatively unimportant to the topic at hand. The point is that even when the specialist is operating at a profit, his inventory might be positioned in such a way that a potentially large loss is virtually certain and vice versa. More importantly his position at any time is subject to radical change almost without notice.

Nevertheless applying the method used to prepare appendix D, it is

Klunky, Inc.
Analysis of Specialist Trading

	Odd Lot		Round Lot	
	Shares	$ Value	Shares	$ Value
Opening inventory	19	$ 627.00	1,400	$ 45,187.00
Plus:				
Purchases made during month	8,754	295,991.62	53,300	1,796,700.50
Total purchases	8,773	$296,618.62	54,700	$1,841,887.50
Less:				
Sales made during month	4,857	$165,551.62	55,200	$1,864,025.00
Closing inventory position	3,916		[500]	
Transfer from odd lot to round lots	[500]	[17,510.75]	500	17,510.75
Net remaining inventory position	3,416		-0-	

Profit-Loss Analysis

Proceeds to specialist on stock he sold		$165,551.62	$1,864,025.00
(FIFO) Cost to specialist of stock he sold		159,474.62	1,859,398.25
Profit from trading operations		$ 6,077.00	$ 4,626.75
Closing inventory and its cost to specialist	3,416	$119,633.25	
Average cost per share of his closing inventory		$35.02	
Month end closing price of Klunky stock		$32.25	
Indicated loss to specialist from inventory account (per share)		$(2.77)	
Indicated loss to specialist from inventory account (in total)		$(9,467.25)	

interesting to note that after turning over 60,057 shares for an indicated trading profit of $10,703.75, the specialist was faced with a con-
tingent loss of $9,467.25 which if realized would have left him with a
profit of only $1,236.50 or less than 2 cents per share before operating
expenses. Assuming this contingency did not actually happen, still
only 29,600 (53.6 per cent) of the shares turned over were done so at
a profit. Of the remaining trades, the specialist lost money on 20,700
(37.5 per cent) and broke even on 4,900 shares (8.9 per cent). His
biggest profit was 2¾ points while his biggest loss was 3⅛ points.

The month started badly for the specialist. He turned over 9,900 shares before breaking even. After trading 10,000 shares his gross trading profit was only $37.50!

At 15,000 shares, his trading profit was an enormous $787.50. By the time he traded 26,200 shares, his profit reached $4,000. Then the market turned against him again. He had a string of 69 consecutive trades where he either lost money or just broke even. At one point during the month, the specialist had a $6,137.50 loss in his round lot account.

This analysis should shatter once and for all the myth that all transactions are automatically profitable to specialists. When they do make money, they often do so for one reason. The nature of their franchise forces them to buy more and more stock as prices decline. In effect they are forced to keep dollar averaging all the way down, even when they themselves might not want to. In contrast, most other investors walk away at this moment of greatest opportunity only to come back later when prices are much higher.

To summarize then, the specialist unit on a FIFO basis earned $14,763.75 from its activities in Klunky stock during a typical month. This came from the following three sources:

Floor brokerage fees	$4,060.00
Round lot trading profits	4,626.75
Odd lot trading profits	6,077.00
Total	$14,763.75

This $14,763.75 is, however, the gross trading profit. From this figure certain fixed operating expenses must be deducted. First there is the matter of taxes and fees. Of these taxes the most important is the New York State Stock Transfer Tax which the specialist, like any other owner of stock, must pay whenever he sells stock. The fee on stock selling at $20.00 or more is 5 cents per share. Reviewing his records we find that the specialist unit sold 60,057 shares of Klunky from its account during the month which, at 5 cents per share, would be $3,002.85.

Another, smaller tax is the Securities Exchange Commission Transactions Fee of 1 cent on each $500 or fraction that is involved in a trade. In Klunky, this would come to about 7 cents on each round lot and anywhere from 1 to 7 cents per odd lot. The expense in this area to the unit would be something under $45.00.

The unit's next expense was the cost of carrying its overnight positions. We saw that the specialist's beginning position was a short position of 1,419 shares and his ending position was 3,416 shares. In between, overnight positions ranged from a high of 7,000 shares to a low of 500 shares. In monetary terms this translates from a high of $235,000 to a low of about $17,000. Their average overnight investment was about $85,000. Under specialist margin rules, 25 per cent of this amount must come from his own funds and he is permitted to borrow the remaining 75 per cent or $63,750. At a going rate of 7 per cent which has been an unrealistically low figure during the early 1970s, interest for one month would be about $375.

Next comes the cost of clearing the transactions. This includes bookkeeping expenses, computer costs, transfer handling charges, billings to brokers for handling their trades and all the other miscellaneous costs that come from running an office. The exact cost of this aspect of the business is difficult to determine. Some specialists relate it to their daily computer summary of the business they transact. They say that every line on their report costs them from $6 to $8 in expenses whether that line is for 10 odd lot shares on which they earn perhaps $1.25, or for a position on which they will eventually gain or lose $1,000. Some specialists say that assuming they could make an ⅛ point on each round lot, anywhere from $6 to $9 would go for the various expenses associated with their business.

Other specialists relate expenses to the amount of gross profits they generate. Larry has stated that in good times when the unit is earning its anticipated levels of profits, clearing charges absorb about a third of his gross profit. Still others have said that these charges can run as high as 50 per cent. All take pains to point out that these are fixed charges that must be paid regardless of how profitable their specializing activities are. Thus even when they lose money on a trade, specialists still have to bear the expense of clearing that trade. A few specialists have their own clearing organizations but most believe it is less expensive for them to farm out this activity to someone else.

All this is confusing, but for illustrative purposes we will calculate clearing charges to be about $1,900.

The unit also has clerical labor costs to pay. Each specialist is required to have at least one clerk to assist him in maintaining his records during floor trading hours. Specialists might also have clerical assistance in the back office to handle necessary correspondence and clear up problems with the clearing agent, brokers, etc. Thus a five man unit might have five clerks on the floor and two employees in the back office. The cost to them for these assistants might well be at least $12,000 per person or $84,000 considering salaries, bonuses, taxes, fringe benefits, etc. Prorating this amount on a monthly basis among the 40 stocks in the unit, the specialist's labor costs on a single stock would be about $175.

There are other indirect costs that might come to another $500 plus one last fee that I shall term the specialist's "franchise fee" for doing business. This is the exchange fee and it amounts to one per cent of each member's net commissions. In this case, the specialists received floor brokerage commissions of $4,906.90 on which they would pay the Exchange $49.07. The indirect costs include among other things the rental of the specialist's position at his post, rental of time clocks, duplicating equipment, etc., as well as the cost of rectifying errors.

Here then is the specialists' monthly statement of profit and loss in Klunky stock.

Statement of Specialist Income and Expense
Typical Month 19___
Klunky Mfg. Co.

Income:		
Floor brokerage commissions		$4,060.00
Round lot trading profits		4,626.75
Odd lot trading profits		6,077.00
Gross income		$14,763.75
Less:		
Estimated Expenses:		
Clearing fees and related back office expenses	$1,900.00	
Taxes and Fees:		
N.Y. State transfer tax	3,000.00	
S.E.C. transactions fee	45.00	
Exchange transactions fee	49.00	
Interest charges on borrowed capital	375.00	
Clerical labor costs	175.00	
Miscellaneous indirect expenses	100.00	5,644.00
Estimated Net Income:		$9,119.75

In contrast to the widely heralded profits of ⅛ point per share, the unit seems to have earned only about $9,100 on the 301,700 round lot and 13,690 odd lot trading volume in which they participated (or about 3 cents per share). Except for the occasional windfall profit, seldom does a specialist do significantly better than this. Sometimes he does worse.

Finally, to put this $9,100 profit in its proper perspective, it is necessary to realize that the profit represents several distinct elements of income to the specialist unit.

First of all, part of this profit represents ordinary salary income.

Everyone who works at a job, just for coming to work every day is entitled to a salary and the specialist is no different in this respect. He should be entitled to a reasonable salary if for no other reason than for performing the clerical function of matching off limit orders left with him by brokers.

Next, a properly structured salary scale allocates a premium salary to jobs that are unusually demanding. Specializing by its nature is one of the most tension-producing, ulcer-creating jobs in the country. In recognition of this a premium pay element of some sort should be added to the base salary.

A third and often overlooked element is the cost of specializing. Not only are there the direct expenses which we have just reviewed but there's the cost of the specialist's seat and the capital contribution each specialist makes to provide his unit with the capital base from which to carry on the unit's business.

Although the cost of memberships has varied over the years, since the late 1960s when most of the present specialists came on board, the average seat probably cost about $150,000. Assuming the current unsettled state of the business and an estimated working career of 30 years, perhaps some thought should be given to the amortization of memberships over the expected term of a specialist's career. Because of the ready marketability of seats in the past, the question of amortization may have been academic but with the revolutionary changes of recent years not yet completed, there is a real question as to how much the future value of a membership will be worth. Therefore, a reserve for at least partial amortization of the seat price might be a prudent idea.

Fourth, the specialist must consider that if he were working as an employee of someone else it would not be necessary for him to make an investment for membership or the additional capital which is his share of a unit's capital. Assuming that his investment in his business is several hundred thousand dollars, he could put that money to work earning risk-free interest if he had a salaried job which didn't require him to invest his own money. At the 8 per cent level of 1970, he could have quit specializing and earned $20,000 per year at no risk at all.

Fifth, the demands of his job force him to borrow huge sums in excess of his own investment to carry overnight positions. Because of the high risk involved in borrowing money to run a business of this nature, a risk premium should be permitted to form a reserve against possible future losses. This risk premium which might be as little as 2 per cent or as much as 5 per cent would amount to somewhere between $5,000 and $12,500 annually.

Adding these five items together, it would seem reasonable to assume that the specialist should be entitled to an income of at least $50,000 per year just to cover a minimum salary of $20,000 plus a reasonable amount to cover the income he is losing by not investing his capital in other risk-free alternative ways.

It seems then that it is only when a specialist has earned in excess of this basic $50,000 that the question of excessive profits, can be raised. Just as a manufacturer is entitled to a profit from the value added to the product he manufactures and a service organization a profit for the services it provides, so too, should a specialist be entitled to a fair profit for his labors and the liquidity he provides America's investors. Certainly a profit of 5 cents per share would probably not be considered excessive and our analysis of Klunky shows that for the month reviewed, this five-cent level was not achieved.

19

The Big Bust

THE SITUATIONS we have discussed so far represent the normal challenges a specialist faces in his day to day market making activities. He often gets a stock like Twinkle that sells off on heavy volume. This requires him to step into the market as buyer to moderate the intensity of the decline. Then in a few hours or days the pressure subsides, buying comes back into the stock and he can work off this accumulated inventory.

So long as both the company and the general stock market stay healthy, there is no substantial risk involved to the specialist. The big dangers and opportunities come when something truly unexpected happens. Such events cause an instant revaluation in market price. If the unexpected permits a specialist to work off a large inventory position, then the·unexpected can be enormously profitable to him. On the other hand, if the unexpected occurs when the specialist is poorly positioned for it, his losses can be disastrous.

This danger is very real when one considers that the specialist generally operates on a 25 per cent margin. That means that for every dollar of inventory he has 25 cents of his own money invested and has borrowed 75 cents. This gives the specialist four times more buying power than his own funds alone would provide. This permits him greater flexibility in meeting the buying and selling waves that constantly hit stocks. With full use of his margin resources, even a modestly capitalized specialist unit that uses its borrowing power to capacity usually has enough money to absorb whatever market pressures it faces.

This reliance on margin works to a specialist's advantage when all his stocks are earning money because the magic of margin makes it possible for him to earn four times as much as he could using just his own funds. The problem with this, however, is that it is a two-edged sword, one which hurts a specialist abnormally when the market turns against him. The reason is that the leverage works against him. Where on the one hand it is possible for a specialist using margin to earn four times as much as he could using his own money, it also causes him to lose four times as much. As a result, with the kind of big numbers the specialists play with, they can sometimes be wiped out almost before they are aware that anything has gone wrong.

Therefore, while every specialist learns to expect from time to time a sell off like the one in Twinkle and learns how to handle it as a prerequisite of staying in business, at the same time even those specialists who claim to have a contempt for money are aware of the consequences of being hit with that one big, ultimate loss. This is the loss that comes unexpectedly, out of nowhere and in the twinkle of an eye can wipe out the result of a lifetime of work.

Here are two specific examples of how unexpected events can sometimes provide a specialist with a windfall. On one occasion a stock opened up 13⅞ points from the previous closing price of 36⅛. This price rise was precipitated because an analyst for a major brokerage house had prepared an extremely bullish institutional report on the company. His report prompted a number of institutional accounts to enter large buy orders at the opening. At the same time it caused prospective sellers to withdraw their offers until they could assess the impact of the buying.

After matching the orders, the specialist saw that he had orders to buy approximately 30,000 shares at the market plus several times that amount at limit prices close to the previous close. To offset this, the specialist could find only one willing seller. However, he was demanding $50 per share! After much discussion it was decided to open at 50 with the specialist selling 13,300 shares, most of it short. Immediately thereafter the sellers, who had earlier withdrawn, rushed to sell causing the stock to drop all the way back to 40¾ at the close.

In the post opening market, these sellers sold a total of 59,800 shares. Again their sell orders created a one-sided market. This time the specialist purchased 33,400 shares giving him a substantial long position to carry forward into the following day. I do not know how the specialist fared on the inventory he carried forward but taking out of context the 13,300 shares he sold at the opening plus about 1,100 shares held at the opening and the additional 9,500 shares he sold durng the trading session, this specialist made a one-day windfall gross profit of about $16,800 before expenses. All because an analyst unexpectedly recommended the purchase of a stock and his recommendation had an immediate impact on investors.

Another windfall occurred at about the same time. In this instance an investor, the widow of the founder of a corporation, decided she wanted to sell some of her stock. She contacted a broker who in turn found an institutional buyer. A mutually agreeable price was set at approximately the closing price of the day. However, because the stock was founder's stock and there is sometimes a question as to whether or not such stock can be sold without first registering it with the S.E.C., the broker passed the certificates to his lawyer for clearance. For whatever reason, it took the counsel about a week to issue his opinion. In the meantime the stock went up over a dozen points.

When the stock was finally cleared, it is uncertain what occurred except that the broker brought the stock down to the specialist to cross at the previously agreed upon price, 12 points below the current market. The specialist knew that the cross had nothing to do with corporate operations and would in all probability immediately make up all or most of the decline. He therefore insisted on and received sufficient stock to cover a moderately large short position as well as enough stock to provide an orderly market to the stock as it rebounded back.

Within a few hours the stock was within a point of its previous level and the specialist was again short because the stock he allocated for himself was not sufficient to satisfy all the buying that was generated that day. Nevertheless, the unexpected windfall gave him a one day trading profit of well over $20,000.

On the other hand, one specialist several years back lost several million dollars so fast he never knew he had even been hit. Coming down the final half of the year, Chester was looking forward to his best year of his career. Then, without warning, he suffered what may have been the single biggest loss any specialist on any exchange ever had to swallow.

If as its critics claim, the specialist system is rigged in favor of the specialist and against everyone else, Chester must wonder to this day what went wrong. He certainly didn't plan the loss. As a specialist, he was one of the best. When his stocks threatened to orbit he never lost his nerve. He never stopped making tight markets. But then, this was the nature of the man. In his drive to be the best, he never seemed to mind taking on big positions or going short 20 or 30,000 shares. As long as his stocks stayed active and people wanted to trade, he believed in his ability to provide close markets.

Unfortunately for Chester he was just too good with a stock that didn't deserve it. This was his downfall. Because he knew he was good, he often took chances that lesser men would have backed away from. He had guts. He had a flair. He had style and he had nerve. Up until the big bust he even had money, plenty of it. His used all his talents in abundance in handling Tek Neek. This was the worst thing he could have done.

At the time, Tek Neek was a speculator's dream. It generally traded at least 10,000 shares a day. Weekly volume was often 200,000 shares or more. With volume this high a specialist need not generally participate to the same extent that he would in a less active stock. Nevertheless, Chaster sometimes carried positions in excess of 50,000 shares. In a stock in Tek Neek's price range, this meant a risk exposure of as much as $2 to $3 million.

While this might seem unduly risky as a point of fact, in a good market with a strongly bullish undertone there can be much less risk to a position of this size than there is with a much smaller position during a bear market. So long as nothing unexpected happens, a high flying stock with volume of this kind actually seems to draw speculators into almost regularly predictable waves of buying and profit taking. If a specialist could anticipate these waves correctly, they could prove immensely profitable to him.

As part of his job it is necessary for the specialist to fill the vacuum caused by these alternating waves. Otherwise, the amplitude of the price swings might be several times greater than the already wide swings some stocks carve for themselves. Therefore, while large positions in active stocks are not necessarily a problem as long as the unexpected does not happen, in the case of Tek Neek, the unexpected did happen.

For 2 weeks the stock was under heavy selling pressure dropping from 62 to 45. During this time over 400,000 shares traded. In the face of this selling, Chester had been a big buyer on balance. According to rumors circulating around the shop, he had an inventory of over 50,000 shares.

Then it happened. It was late on a Friday afternoon, almost at the closing. A broker brought an order to sell 50,000 shares at market! The stock was trading at 45. Although it was an active number, there was nowhere near 50,000 shares to buy regardless of price. In fact the bid side had almost been wiped out by the selling pressures of the past few weeks. In view of his already large position Chester didn't have the kind of money required to buy the block. As a result he requested and received permission to halt trading until the following Monday because of the selling influx.

He hoped to find both buyers and additional funds to take on the block while the trading halt was in effect but something about the reaction of previous sponsors of the stock alerted him to the fact that the company was in serious trouble. The stock that hit the Floor that Friday afternoon was not an ordinary block (to the extent that any 50,000 share block of stock is "ordinary"). The stock offered for sale that day was being dumped by the company's management. They had overextended themselves manipulating the price of their stock through a number of secret accounts in an effort to raise its price. Now, all the chickens were coming home to roost.

Through their manipulative efforts the price of the stock appreciated significantly. This, in turn, enabled them to make acquisitions on what appeared to be very attractive terms by using highly inflated stock. Now the bubble was about to burst. Brokers and bankers concerned with the loss in collateral value of the stock in recent weeks were calling for more margin in the secret accounts. But management was already overextended. They had taken advantage of all money sources available to them. Their only recourse was to dump stock on the market even if this caused it to drop still further. They had come to the end of their rope. This was the only way to go.

Had Chester known this, he never would have gone home that day so complacent and unconcerned. Indeed at the time, his only concern was that this block had come at a time when he already had such a large position that he could not buy it immediately without having to resort to a halt in trading.

The weekend passed. Fortunately Chester was not able to borrow immediately the additional money he needed. To have done so would only have compounded an already impossible situation. As a result the trading halt continued. When the stock did not reopen, rumors started to fly. They were so incessant that they even reached those of us on the staff who generally heard rumors only after the last odd-lotter has heard it.

In tracking down the rumors, one thing led to another until ultimately the facts behind the manipulation were confirmed. As soon as the Exchange satisfied itself that a manipulation had in fact taken place, the temporary trading halt was changed to a longer lasting suspension in order to give time to gather all the facts needed to clarify the situation.

At the same time the S.E.C. suspended the stock from trading over-the counter leaving the specialist caught holding the bag along with everyone else. He was boxed into a position he could not liquidate thereby freezing his assets.

Without having access to his personal trading records, it is impossible to know precisely how much Chester lost on this catastrophe but it was in excess of one million dollars. As a tribute to the resiliency of the human spirit, Chester, recovered from the tragedy and still functions as a specialist although if anyone were to bet on it, it would be safe to assume that he is no longer, nor will he ever attempt to be the boldest specialist in the industry.

Of course what happened to Chester is not typical. Hopefully this kind of thing doesn't happen more than once every two or three generations. But it can happen, it has happened, and undoubtedly it will happen again. As a result, the fear of loss is a very real fact in the thinking of the specialist. Also real are the smaller but more significant losses in the area of $20,000 to $100,000 or more from which virtually no specialist is immune because of the regularity with which they occur. These losses might not wipe out a specialist but they do long and irreparable damage to his ability to do business. In the 1969–1970 bear market many losses of this magnitude occurred as institutions and others rushed to dump indiscriminately stocks that either disappointed them or just failed to live up to their fondest delusions.

Because this overhanging fear of loss is so real and because such large sums of money have to be invested, the compensating profits to the specialist by necessity have to be large. Whether or not they are sufficiently large enough to compensate for the risks and expenses attendant to the business is another question. Obviously to the extent that people are willing to enter or remain in this business they at least feel the rewards override the risks.

While the unexpected can be a disaster for a specialist, it can sometimes create a windfall for him. The biggest windfall will wipe out the losses of a year or more. Sometimes it will even make him an instant millionaire. The biggest windfall in recent years was the one all specialists shared together on August 16, 1971, the day after President Nixon imposed the freeze on both prices and wages, restricted the export of gold and took other measures designed to bolster the economy and bring inflation to a halt.

Just prior to this day, the market had been in a downtrend for about 4 months. The Dow Jones Industrial Index which had recovered handsomely from the crash of May, 1970 had dropped over a 100 points from its recovery high and analysts were once again concerned that a new bear market was in the process of unfolding. Under these conditions, selling had begun to accelerate, forcing ever increasing positions of stock on specialists who were looking for a rally in order to work off their inventories.

This announcement by the president gave the specialists the opportunity they were looking for. It brought a tremendous surge of buyers into the market. The need to meet this surge enabled them to clean out inventories accumulated in prior weeks.

Volume on the day was 31.7 million shares on the N.Y.S.E. and over 10 million on the Amex. The Dow Jones Index was up almost 33 points recouping in just one day over a third of the loss of the previous 4 months.

The demand to buy was so great that most specialists not only were able to sell most of their accumulated inventories at some of the most favorable trading profits in years, but they then turned around and went short at levels sufficiently high so as to virtually guarantee good trading profits when the time came to cover their shorts.

Demand was so extensive that morning that a study released by the New York Stock Exchange shows that 10 of the 31 million shares traded during the day were at the opening. Of these 10 million opening block shares, the market was so unbalanced that specialists sold 3.6 million shares for their own account. During the day, they not only sold 3.7 million shares they had accumulated during the decline but they went short an additional 4.3 million shares.

Dozens of stocks opened 2, 3, even 10 points above the previous Friday's close, resulting in trading profits counted not in pennies but in dimes and dollars.

20

Who Needs Him?

INDEPENDENT OF any other activity at the post, there is virtually always a small crowd near Will Leifer. Their interest centers around a stock with the letters GAS. No, this isn't the symbol of a manufacturer of antacid pills. Instead GAS is the symbol of a large Canadian mineral exploration firm whose stock trades both on the Amex and in Toronto. The stock enjoys periodic bursts of high volume, much of it due to arbitrage activity between the two Exchanges.

The men currently in the GAS crowd represent arbitragers. An arbitrager is, of course, a man who arbitrages. If you look up the word in your dictionary the odds are you won't find it unless you have one of those foot thick authoritative editions. But if you got the drift of the discussion when we were talking about how market orders cause prices to move in a direction away from the pressure, then you can understand that it's possible for a stock like GAS to be rising in price in Toronto in response to someone buying there, while at precisely the same time it is falling on Amex because someone is selling. An arbitrager knowing this, keeps his eyes on the two prices. Whenever he sees a disparity in the price, he attempts to profit from the disparity and in the process get the stock's price on the two exchanges back into balance again. When done correctly this is virtually a risk-free transaction. For this reason the arbitrager will do his work for a potential profit of pennies provided that he can turn over sufficient shares in the process. To save on expenses, most arbitagers are stock exchange members. They trade through member firm trading accounts which means they pay no brokerage commissions.

Here's how arbitraging works. Let's assume that at this moment GAS is trading on Amex at $20 per share and it is in approximate parity in Toronto. If it is trading at the same price in Toronto as it is on Amex, it does not follow that the price of GAS in Toronto will also be $20. The reason is that at any given moment a Canadian dollar might be worth more or less than an American dollar. The difference might not be much, it might only be a fraction of a penny, but nevertheless it is a factor that the arbitrager must take into consideration.

For the sake of our example, let's assume that the spread today is a fairly wide 8 cents in favor of the Canadian dollar. This means that for an American $1.00 you can buy only 92 Canadian cents. Therefore, if GAS was selling at $20 on the Amex, the equivalent Toronto price would have to be $18.40. However, since stocks trade in eighths and quarters the stock in Toronto is most likely to have last traded at 18⅜. With this difference of only 2½ cents per share no arbitrage is likely to occur because even without paying commissions there are other expenses involved and their cost is greater than the price spread at this moment (thus making it impractical to arbitrage).

However, if a thousand-share order to sell were to hit the market, an opportunity to arbitrage might occur. If the thousand-share order came on the Amex Floor the seller might get 19¾; in Toronto he might get 18⅛. In both cases the selling would cause the market to drop ¼ point. If the order was shown on Amex, one of the brokers in the crowd would try to buy the stock for 19¾, then immediately attempt to resell it in Toronto. The Canadian equivalent price of 19¾ is $18.17. Therefore, the ability to successfully sell the stock in Toronto for either 18¼ or 18⅜ will bring a profit to the arbitrager. On the other hand, if the trade came to the Toronto floor, the arbitrager would attempt to buy it there, then immediately try to resell it on Amex for any price between 19¾ and 20. If after the initial trade a disparity still exists, that is, if after buying the stock on one market, then reselling it on the other, the price difference on the two markets is more than 2 or 3 pennies, additional trades will occur until the prices on both exchanges are once again approximately equal. In the process, then, of attempting to capitalize on natural swings in the market place, the arbitrager's activities serve to keep prices of dually traded stocks approximately equal at all times.

The men in the GAS crowd are not themselves arbitragers. Instead, they are brokers representing arbitragers. The arbitrager himself sits at a telephone console somewhere with lines open to both Amex and Toronto. Any time a broker approaches Will with an order of any kind, these men in the crowd attempt to overhear the conversation. Then, using hand signals, they relay what they hear to their clerk who in turn transmits it by phone to the arbitrager. In Toronto a similar process is taking place. Thus the arbitrager is at all times fully apprised of the activity in both markets. He is, in fact, even more fully informed than the specialist because the specialist knows only the situation in his market. The arbitrager is aware not only of all transactions but he knows of all bids and offers to hit both markets as well as all quotation changes. If something occurs to trigger the arbitrager, he simultaneously enters his offsetting orders on both exchanges where he gets virtually instantaneous executions.

One arbitrage broker estimates that often as much as 40 per cent of all reported volume of stocks trading here and in Tonronto is handled by arbitragers. Commenting on proposed changes in the way of doing business, he said, "There is a lot of talk these days about doing away with the specialist and putting the market on a computer. The people pushing for this, claim it would increase the efficiency of the market but my own observation is that it will create more problems than it will solve. I know it will kill the arbitrage business and in the process it will cause wider price disparities to develop. This will be especially likely if permission were granted for specialists to openly compete with each other in maintaining markets in the same stock. When that happens you will open virtually every stock to arbitrage which I am for but at the same time the computer will make it more difficult to conduct an efficient arbitrage.

"Although there are perhaps 50 or more Canadian stocks with dual markets, only about a half dozen are active at any one time. To keep the prices of these few stocks in line on both exchanges keeps about 30 people busy full time. Even then we occasionally miss something. At the present time, there are about a half dozen firms involved in arbitrage. Each firm has a broker and a clerk here on the Floor, another broker and clerk in Toronto as well as someone to do the actual arbitraging back in the office.

"If the auction process were to be completely computerized, much of our sensitivity to the market and our speed in executing orders would be lost. We now work so swiftly and efficiently that in less time than it takes to punch out a quote and have it appear on his screen our man cannot only get quotes from the two markets but executions as well. Therefore, forcing him to work exclusively with a computer will slow things down considerably.

"Working strictly with a computer would also give him a much poorer feel for the quality of the market. For instance, he knows that as of this moment there are three of us working on GAS here. He also knows how active the interest is in Toronto. If all this was computerized he would have no way of knowing the degree of interest that exists. My man has been working both sides of the market but he is a small buyer on balance. One of the other brokers is also a buyer while the third is a seller. I suspect the fellow who is buying is doing so because his arbitrager is stuck with a short position and the market looks higher. Earlier in the day he sold a block here to a house that deals mainly with institutions. Apparently he planned to cover the sale with a block that was being shopped in Montreal. However, before he could wash his sale with the Montreal block, we bought it for one of our customers. Now with the market looking stronger, he's starting to get a little nervous. The seller looked as though he was going to dump his stock but when he saw the two of us buying, he advised his client and got instructions not to offer the stock but to work the order off against bids.

"With the market organized as it is at the present time, it is relatively simple for me and for any good broker to get a feel for the quality as well as the size of the market at any particular time. This gives our customers a better feel of the market than they will ever have with a computerized auction. For instance, currently the market is being quoted 20 to an eighth, 300 by 500 but that is not the true market because I know the buyer competing with me is still short about 7,000 shares which he is going to have to cover one way or another. In addition I've overheard several people at the post recently inquiring about the availability of stock in moderate size. The specialist indicated he thought there might be some available if the market moved up a little. This means he either has orders on his book to sell up about a point or so or someone has told him they are interested sellers should a firm bid come in above the present market. In addition, the third broker in the crowd is an active seller but not a nervous one. He hasn't given an indication of the size of his selling nor has he done anything to put pressure on the market price, yet.

"I honestly don't see how we are going to operate if all we will have to work with will be the disclosed size and quote from a computer. On balance I think the end result will be much less trading coupled with much greater volatility because it will be so difficult to sound out the market.

"Then again, with me on the Floor, my arbitrager has a window on anything that might develop. I know the stocks he generally works. Although I'm concentrating on GAS right now, I know where the others are located. If I see a crowd develop at any post where his stocks trade, I get the word to him immediately. On the other hand, if all he had to rely on was a computer screen and if he was concentrating on a particular stock it could be quite some time before he would know that something was happening in some other stock."

I was aware of many of the arguments for preserving the specialist system from the specialist's point of view but until this conversation, I never gave much thought to how the Floor Broker who is the specialist's natural adversary viewed the system. From this conversation it appeared that they too considered the present system of vital benefit to their customers.

"Certainly the present form of auction market works best for my customers" says another broker. "Being down here on the Floor gives me a feel for the market that I can relay to those of my customers who want to know. This is something a computer will not be able to do. Most larger orders are not disclosed on the book. The specialist and sometimes other brokers know that they are around but for obvious reasons advertising them by putting them on the book would be counterproductive. People would tend to work against the order. Therefore, it is rare that the specialist has over 1,000 shares to buy or sell on his book at any time. At the same time, often many times this amount is available to trade at or very close to the current market. The specialist is usually aware of these blocks and is ready to help with their execution. Therefore by talking to a specialist and analysing his reactions to your inquiry, even though he cannot disclose the condition of his book, it is still possible to get a good reaction of what the market can accommodate at any particular time. With the computer I will know what is on the book at the quoted market but unless people choose to disclose their orders more readily than at present, I will lose my feel for the true depth of the market. Certainly the computer might be able to handle the mechanical aspects of trading as well or better than the current system but I doubt that, because there have already been so many technical market improvements in' the past dozen years.

"Because I have such a good feel for the market, I never automatically execute an order the way it is entered if it is a sizeable order. Instead I size up the market first. For instance, if I have a buy order and a specialist tells me there are no sell orders on his book but that he expects some shortly, I might ask my customer to consider changing his instructions. Then, instead of entering a market order and forcing the price of the stock up I try to use some discretion in working it off against incoming sell orders. It is possible that the anticipated sell orders will not appear and that my customers might eventually pay a higher price but as a rule they generally do much better."

Away from the Floors where much less is known about the mechanical operations of the auction process, suggestions for change have been much more radical. Often whenever a discussion turns to the specialist and his role in the market, someone will invariably ask, "Who needs him?"

Because of the almost universal need for a scapegoat on whom to heap abuse for their stock market failures, investors and registered representatives have turned to the specialist because he is someone deeply involved in the process yet conveniently removed from themselves. In such eyes, the specialist is unreliable at best, probably dishonest, possibly worse. As unrealistic as such a belief is, many investors succeed in deluding themselves into believing that the unprofitable investments they so enthusiastically made were engineered by the specialist for his own personal benefit. One sometimes hears, "If he had not run the stock up, I never would have bought it." Investors seldom seem to consider that it is their own eagerness to buy or sell that is a vital pressure affecting the direction of the market at any particular moment.

Even some corporate officials who should know better complain about poor specialist performance when their only "proof" is that the price of their stock is down. Therefore, critics reason, some other means of trading stocks ought to be devised. Often the same corporate official who lauded his specialist in 1968, when his stock sold in excess of 50 times earnings for providing great stability to the market, cursed him in 1970 when the stock was selling at 10 to 20 times greatly reduced earnings. At these lower prices the specialist often was performing a statistically better job in supporting the market but few care to recognize this.

Corporate complaints invariably arise because of a psychological difficulty in divorcing the performance of their stock from the performance of their company; or during times when a company is losing money, of divorcing the price of their stock from its book value if that happens to be higher. The price of a stock is a personal thing to them, especially when they own large blocks of it which might be in hock at some bank. Therefore, it is difficult to reconcile to the fact that once they have sold stock to the public, that stock was transformed into a commodity, the price of which is determined by many factors of which the performance of the company is just one.

On the one hand they think improving corporate performance should be directly translatable into a rising stock price even in weak markets. They become disappointed with their specialist when this does not follow. On the other hand if their stock is selling above a reasonable level (it's never too high) and then recedes, or when the price drops because of adverse operating reports, the specialist is vilified for permitting the drop in price. In the eyes of many people the market should only rise. The specialist should then be obligated to buy all stock offered for sale at the highest price attained. To these people, any market system which permits the price of a stock to drop for whatever reason is an inherently evil one which should be replaced at the earliest possible moment.

Critics of the present specialist system appear to be divided into some variation of two alternatives. On the one hand, there are those who advocate that a specialist system could operate much more effectively if there are competing specialists while others argue that the market will be better served if the specialist were done away with and replaced with a computer. While it may be true that in some respects the mechanical handling of market transactions might be improved by the implementation of these two ideas, there are a number of possible adverse consequences that investors should be aware of.

The reason advanced for competing specialists is that they will provide greater depth to the market. The rationale advanced is that "since most specialists only make 100-share markets when they have no orders, two specialists would automatically double the depth at each price level." The idea is that with each specialist buying 100 shares at each price level, a given volume of orders would only affect market volatility half as much as it now does.

This does not necessarily follow. First of all, we have already seen that specialists on both exchanges do in practice provide more than 100-share markets in most stocks, most of the time. Therefore, the argument starts with an improper premise. But assuming that the basic premise was correct, it still would not automatically follow that market depth would be multiplied by a system of competing specialists.

To begin with, when markets are active and stocks are advancing on heavy volume, the high level of activity automatically gives a stock the benefits that would accrue from multiple specialists. Everyone wants to trade active rising stocks making the question of depth academic. Actually some people might view too much depth as detrimental at such times because this would keep a stock from rising in price too fast. Therefore, in rising markets a dual specialist system might or might not help things but it probably wouldn't hurt anything.

However, when prices are falling or in inactive stocks, a dual specialist system might actually be detrimental. As it now stands, specialists complain that the principal reason for apparently poor markets in most stocks lies with the thinness of the book. To attempt to change the situation here would only worsen the situation because it would fragment an already poor market even more. If anything, the situation in many stocks is deteriorating because of the tendency for institutions to first buy out the stock of numerous individuals in a series of small transactions. Then, having dried up the market and driven away all interested investors, they expect to sell en masse in a series of large block trades. When they attempt to sell in the face of non-existing buyers, they complain about the poor quality of the auction process. But this is a monster they themselves created. Actually, if the truth were known, given the opportunity and knowing that the action would not prejudice his actions, virtually every specialist unit has several stocks they would gladly give up to anyone who wanted to take them on.

There is a time, however, when competing specialists would be very detrimental to a stock. With competing specialists there might be a tendency to walk away from a stock at precisely the times the support of a specialist is needed the most. These times are when volume and trading interest is low thus making it difficult to make good trading markets and again during panic periods when people are indiscriminately dumping stocks and specialists are being called on to take inordinately large inventory positions.

Can't you just picture the jurisdictional disputes that are likely to arise? Someone wants to sell 1,000 shares. There are no bids on either specialists' book and neither specialist wants to buy the stock. Specialist A says it's now B's turn to buy because he took in the last trade of 100 shares. B on the other hand is arguing that with blocks each broker should be required to purchase 500 shares. I don't see how it will be possible to force a specialist to take on inventory positions he doesn't want under these circumstances. It is sometimes difficult enough now, with responsibility centered on just one party to enforce the "affirmatve obligation" of specialists to buy. With dual specialists it might be almost impossible. At such times a specialist's activities might well center on finding techniques to force sellers to sell to his competitor.

A system of dual specialists might also make it possible to change the level of prices without the direct interaction of supply and demand. At the present time a specialist is required to maintain price continuity. That is the specialist is supposed to see to it that prices of stocks move only in response to actual orders. He is also obligated to insure that each price change is nominal and reasonable in relation to the price of the stock and the size of the order. Thus if he gets an order to sell a 100 shares of stock at a time when the highest bid is 14 and the last sale was at 15, as we have seen he is obligated to buy the stock himself, probably at 14¾ or 14⅞.

However, with competing specialists, if the rules were not correctly drawn, it might be possible for a specialist to arbitrarily change his quotation other than in response to market forces as over-the-counter dealers now do. In the process, rather than modifying volatility, greater volatility might well result.

The reality of competing specialists then, instead of providing stronger markets could well signal a throwback to the "good old days" when stock prices could be manipulated from the Floor. Should this be forced on the market, much of the effort since 1962 to institute effective market controls and tighten the market process might be nullified. The dual specialist system might well reverse the trend toward tighter quotation while at the same time encourage increased price variations between trades and greater over-all price volatility.

The strongest arguments favoring competing specialists have been advanced by institutional spokesmen. The feeling seems to be that because of the large volume of business they transact, it would be possible for institutional accounts to play one specialist against another to force a better execution of their orders much as they now play one broker against another. But the economics of the broker and the specialist differ. Anyone who has done any securities business recently knows that a broker can earn as much as $50 gross on each 100-share order. As we have seen, the specialist must content himself with a gross of $6 to $12. Often he does worse. Therefore, to begin with, the money is just not there from the specialist's point of view. He cannot afford to cut corners in response to customer pressures the way a broker can.

Next, institutional investors conveniently choose to ignore the fact that execution of their orders often creates the disruptive market problems of which they and others complain. When institutions decide to focus in on a stock, their buying can dry up the bulk of the available floating supply. That is what permits them to drive up the price of the stock in the first place. But it also frightens away the value oriented investor. After all, why should he buy a stock at $50 that he earlier sold at $20? Therefore when the institution decides to sell, it finds itself dumping stock into a vacuum it alone created. This pattern of trading has created severe problems to specialists with the result that they have been increasingly reluctant and unable to bail the institutions out.

Now, instead of trying to strengthen the market place, their mistaken solution is to fragment it still more. Unfortunately this will only compound the problem. A specialist who finds it difficult to operate profitably in a disruptive atmosphere when he has all the business will find it doubly difficult to operate when his business is fragmented. Thus the institution might well find that when it goes to sell, rather than having one specialist to play against the other, there will be two parties both trying to jockey themselves out of having to deal with the institution. Under these circumstances, the price of liquidity could be very high for the institution.

Just as a competitive specialist system has its drawbacks during periods when it is most desperately needed, so too does a fully computerized auction program have its drawbacks, some of which have already been discussed.

First of all, some way is going to have to be developed to insure that the specialist's functions and obligation to buy and sell are pro-grammed into the system. Then it is going to be necessary to sell the system to the specialists. Specialists have voiced an understandable reluctance to put their money out at risk at the discretion of a computer program which they had no voice in programming. Understand-ably, they prefer to trade on the basis of their own judgement believ-ing they know best how to decide the strategy under which their assets are going to be deployed. Many specialists insist a computer program can never fill their function successfully. There are too many variables they say that cannot all be neatly programmed. Even those specialists willing to concede that an automated specialist system might work say they want someone else to try it first.

Again, assuming this problem can be resolved, others equally serious remain. There is the problem of how to reveal to the computer that you are interested in trading without actually putting an order on the book. There is the problem of finding out how much of this unre-vealed interest is available whenever someone wants to actively buy or dispose of a block. Currently, the specialist can usually give the broker an indication but a computer might not be able to monitor this contingent interest.

Because it may not be possible to get an accurate feel for the market an entirely different approach to trading will of necessity evolve. This will be especially true for institutions. It will probably become neces-sary to enter more and larger limit orders while at the same time reducing the number of market orders entered. It may be impossible to negotiate with the computer as one now does with the specialist.

Computerizing the auction process might open up the information contained in the system to unauthorized parties. This could have a detrimental effect on honest investors and the market in general.

If too much sensitivity is lost, a computerized auction might force even greater numbers of investors with blocks to sell to shop the block outside the organized market. Ironically, while today under the present system trading quoted stocks away from the Exchange is often detrimental to the most efficient operation of the auction process, a completely automated market might produce the opposite results. It might well be that a fully automated central market might create so much volatility that for self-preservation, block traders will of neces-sity be forced to trade on a clandestine over-the-counter market.

This will raise a danger both to smaller investors and to companies alike because the more business that is transacted away from the

Exchange and the watchful eyes of Exchange surveillance teams, the more difficult it will be to detect and halt illegal market activities.

In answer then to the question of who needs him, it would appear that an experienced, closely supervised specialist exercising his honest judgment to provide an orderly market is in everybody's best interests until a demonstratably better system is devised. Despite the acknowledged flaws and the criticisms that have been leveled against him, the specialist has served the needs of the investment community for many years. Any proposed changes should first be carefully considered and tested rather than rashly legislated into existence only to be nullified after the changes have caused the collapse of our economic system.

21

Is Anybody Watching?

CRITICS OF the specialist system have observed correctly that the specialist in his multiple capacity as agent for others and as dealer and trader for his own account has the potential for private personal gain at the expense of investors who entrust orders to him.

This potential for public harm would be especially serious if there were no procedures in effect to monitor the specialist's' trading activity or to supervise the manner in which they may trade for their own personal accounts. Fortunately for investors, some very sophisticated procedures are in effect at the Amex to monitor each and every transaction that occurs. The Amex became the first auction in history to monitor every trade that takes place on its premises. To its credit, is the fact that it wanted to initiate such a system and make it effective.

Its surveillance activities are designed not just to protect the public from the specialist, or vice versa, but to protect each major segment of stock market participants from improperly or illegally taking advantage of any other segment. Everything the specialist himself does is automatically reviewed. Proof of that can be seen by the illustrations in this book. If the specialist was not supervised, his activities could not have been so minutely detailed. At the same time everything surrounding any particular market transaction can be completely reconstructed when necessary. It is possible for the Exchange, if necessary, to determine the names and addresses of every buyer and seller of every share of stock along with the relevant details surrounding each order.

The records that are automatically produced by the Exchange coupled with those the specialist himself must provide give the Exchange a most comprehensive picture of his activities. These make it possible for the staff to work with precise data, not vague assumptions whenever a question comes up as to the propriety of the market at any given time. This control of the market process from specialist to customer makes it extremely difficult for anyone involved in a transaction to hide for long anything improper or illegal once attention is focused on the transaction.

The most important single report used by the Exchange in its market supervisory efforts is an electronically prepared daily journal. This journal summarizes by stock everything that was entered on to the exchange ticker and quotation networks during the day. The main body of this report consists of eight columns, the first four of which pertain to the quotations transmitted to brokerage offices. These columns show the time, bid, offer and spread between the bid and offer for every quotation made by the specialist and entered into the quotation network during the day.

Columns five through eight are a summary of the sales as they appeared on the ticker tape during the day. These columns show the time each trade was flashed on the ticker tape, the volume of shares traded, the price and the amount of price change or variation from the trade which immediately preceded it.

Following this is a summary of market activity showing the total number of shares traded during the day, the total number of trades and the average number of shares per transaction.

This in turn is followed by a summary of all market activity broken down by the amount of price change beween the trade in question and the preceding trade. This section also records the average price difference between each trade recorded during the day. This report glaringly highlights any transaction which caused the price of the stock to fluctuate alarmingly.

Accompanying this Daily Journal Report is an exceptions report

Daily Journal Report—04/05/73 Pg 55

Argyle Corportion—ARG Post 07 Specialist—Harkins-Leifer (357) 1460

Time	Quoted	Market	Spread	Time Prior Close	Volume	Price	Variation	Specialist Purchases R/L	O/L	Participation Sales R/L	O/L
					36					S-2,084	
9:55	36	36½	½								
10:00	36	36¼	¼								20
				10:03	200	36¼	+½			100	
10:03	36	36½	½								
10:17	36	36¼	¼						75		
				10:25	100	36¼	+0				
10:27	36	36½	½								
11:20	36	36⅜	⅜								
				11:52	100	36¼	+0			100	
12:15	36	36¼	¼								
				12:23	100	36¼	+0				
12:25	36	36⅜	⅜								
1:48	36	36¼	¼								
1:51	36	36½	½								
2:50	36	36¼	¼								
				3:00	600	36¼	+0				

1,100 Shares Traded   5 Trades   220 Average Shares Per Trade

At each variation

	unch.	⅛	¼	⅜	½	⅝	¾	⅞	1	1+
Trades	4	0	1	0	0	0	0	0	0	0
(Cum. pct.)	80.0%		100.0%							
Shares	900	0	200							
(Cum. pct.)	81.8%		100.0%							

Average Variation $.050

At each spread

	unch.	⅛	¼	⅜	½	⅝	¾	⅞	1	1+
Quotes	0	0	5	2	4	0	0	0	0	0
(Cum. pct.)	0	0	45.4%	63.6%	100.0%	0	0	0	0	0

Average Spread $.364

For a detailed description on how to read and interpret the information on this daily journal report, please refer to Appendix H.

showing all the trades the computer picked up during the day which caused a stock to swing beyond certain predetermined levels allowed for that stock. This list is available to the staff when they get to work on the day following the activity in question. The report gives them an opportunity to zero in directly without wasting any time on those stocks where price movements between individual trades or in a brief series of consecutive trades appear on the surface to have been excessive.

A typical variation report might show a $5 stock in which the specialist allowed a ¼ point move twice during the day on volume of just 100 shares. For a stock in the five-dollar bracket any move in excess of ⅛ point is reviewed to determine its propriety.

In conducting his review, the analyst will take into consideration a number of things. He will note the price of the stock, its recent average trading volume, its volume on the day in question, the float in the stock, the specialist's position at the time of the trade, the condition of the open order book at the time, etc.

If it is determined that a specialist turned in a poor performance, appropriate action is taken against him. This might range from merely bringing the situation to the attention of the specialist to remind him of the Exchange's constant watchfulness or he may be fined, suspended, lose a stock or even be stricken of his membership.

Most exceptions picked up now that the program has been in effect for a number of years are explainable satisfactorily once all the facts are known. However, even where there sometimes seems to be no justification for a poor specialist performance a reason can often be found from the human side of the picture.

For example a computer once picked up several seemingly unjustifiable transactions by a specialist who shortly after attaining membership became one of the stars on the Floor. As a matter of course his markets were quite professional and very well run. But on this particular day he seemed to have fallen apart for no good reason. A discussion with the specialist revealed he had a serious personal problem that day which carried over to the markets he made.

In recent years, specialists as a group have turned in a 98 to 99 per cent record of stabilization as compared to stabilizing averages of approximately 78 per cent in 1963 on the Amex and 83½ per cent on the N.Y.S.E. in the same year.

Therefore, while it appear at first glance that the rules requiring the specialist to buy stocks at consecutively lower prices while selling from his inventory at consecutively higher prices are designed only to guarantee him trading profits, actually a broader social good is served and the temptation to manipulate the price level of stocks is effectively controlled.

In the 1950's and prior, before this requirement came into effect, it appeared to be standard practice for some specialists to trade without regard to the desirability of stabilizing the market. A specialist who wanted to move his stocks could, for instance, initiate trades himself by buying up the offerings on his book at successively higher prices and stepping ahead of orders left with him in the process. It is for this reason that so many vitriolic comments concerning specialists were made in the past.

Today the specialist cannot initiate a trade or change the direction of a trend by trading in his own account. Therefore when he does make a profit, it is usually well-deserved because of the risks he takes employing his resources for the broader social good.

When it comes to the few transactions that a specialist affects on destabilizing trades, the staff looks to see that they were made in accordance with certain strict restrictions.

For instance, a specialist might have been forced into a large inventory position because of abnormal selling in a stock. In one such situation I recall the specialist had accumulated a position of almost 17,000 shares in a stock which usually traded less than 1,500 shares per week. Under normal conditions it might take him 6 months to work off this amount of stock.

Under these conditions, if the specialist received a large limit order to buy stock just under the market, he might, because of the circumstances, receive permission to sell some of his stock to this bidder.

An occasion where a specialist is permitted to buy on destabilizing ticks might involve an instance where he knows large buying interest is likely soon which will drive the price of the stock much higher. To accumulate enough inventory to modify this expected rise he is sometimes permitted to purchase inventory if a block of stock is offered for sale.

For instance, a specialist might have a stock which has huge overhead resistance at $20. Everytime the stock rises to this level it stops dead in its tracks. Now, however, he sees that a small group of persons are buying all the stock being dumped on the market at the resistance area. At the same time, he senses that the amount of stock being offered at $20 is less than that offered in the past. It looks as though this time, the stock finally will sell above $20. If it does, on technical buying alone, he has reason to believe that a strong demand for the stock will materialize.

Under these circumstances, the specialist might be permitted to buy a portion of the stock being offered at $20 even though it means buying on an uptick. But only if he is short or has a nominal long position; and then only if there is a lack of offers above $20. Because of a lack of offers the stock would tend to be highly volatile except for heavy participation by the specialist.

Although the specialist is permitted to buy stock at such resistance levels, most specialists prefer not to take advantage of the opportunity. "It's really a sucker's game in most cases," explains Larry. "Most of the time when a stock hits a resistance area you will find it will be stopped dead in its tracks. If you do buy, what you end up doing is acting like any average investor which is what a good specialist is supposed to avoid. You wind up involuntarily assisting the people who are trying to break through the resistance area. This is bad because you're not supposed to get emotionally involved with any of your stocks. Then when the breakout attempt fails, you end up with egg on your face and a big inventory position which you bought at the top dollar just like the proverbial odd lotter.

"This idea of buying stock in anticipation of a rise also brings on questions of potential conflict of interest when reviewed by the staff or the S.E.C. if for any reason they decide to conduct an investigation of the stock at a later date. To them my activity undoubtedly will look suspicious even though it was well-intentioned at the time. Since this brings on problems I don't need, unless I absolutely must take on or sell off stock as a matter of economic survival, I try never to get involved in any destabilizing trades."

Even when the quality of the market is not questioned, the specialist's book is reviewed routinely to check against the possibility of his destabilizing the market as well as to independently verify the accuracy of his entries. In conjunction with other data available to the staff, the entries in the specialist's book reveal the extent to which he might be overtrading or refusing to trade adequately in stocks assigned to him.

These and numerous other statistics are maintained to insure the high quality of all specialists' performances. What this means to the investor is that today, even a specialist who might tend to be below average in performance invariably does a much better job than even the best specialists were doing 10 years ago. Consequently, the price variation between consecutive trades is only about 9.6 cents.

The specialist's average rate of participation also has increased from 10 per cent to about 18 per cent in recent years. This has often been a difficult, one-sided participation. For instance, in 1968, much of his participation consisted of shorting the stocks as the market moved up and many stocks were going into orbit. Then when the market declined severely in 1970 and again in late 1971, and everyone tried to sell at once, his participation consisted mostly of buying huge amounts of stock.

The most important thing for the public to remember on a regulated exchange such as the Amex is that someone is watching, and watching very carefully, to insure that the market is fair, orderly and honest.

Not only are the specialists operating on the Amex closely supervised but no one who in any way either directly or indirectly uses the facilities of the Exchange can hope to operate in a vacuum.

In all, about half the 600 people employed by the Exchange are involved in some aspect of monitoring market activity if one stretches the definition of what the word monitoring means. Most of this number devotes all their time to market supervision while the rest either work part time on such activities or they are in some aspect of the work relating to but not directly involved in supervsion.

In addition to supervising the activities of specialists, the staff is concerned with the mechanical operation of the auction process itself. They want to make sure investors have the best, fairest, auction market possible. They try to insure that everyone who uses the facilities of the Exchange does so in an honest, reputable fashion. Thus, the Exchange concerns itself not only with specialists and members, but also with member firms, registered representatives, listed companies, investors and market analysts and commentators as well.

It is within the self-regulating power of the Exchange to discipline Exchange members and their employees. When it comes to others, any information of possible wrongdoing by investors, officers of listed companies or others is first reviewed thoroughly, then turned over to appropriate disciplinary bodies such as the Securities and Exchange Commission or the federal or state attorney general having the required jurisdiction.

Thus the number of disciplinary proceedings reported in newspapers involving Amex stocks is not a reflection that there is rampant wrongdoing on the Amex as some people are wont to believe. Instead it is a tribute to the effectiveness of the Amex staff in uncovering most of the wrongdoing that does occur.

Actually, I am convinced that very little wrongdoing occurs on the Amex, or on any other securities market for that matter. Most securities transactions take place between two parties, both of whom have acted legitimately in all respects.

To illustrate how the Exchange approaches this problem of unusual trading, here is a sequence that once was picked up for review.

Time	Volume	Price	Variation	Flag
11:13	200	21¼	+¼	
11:19	400	21⅜	+⅛	
11:20	900	21½	+⅛	
11:20	1,300	21⅞	+⅜	
11:20	2,500	22¼	+⅜	
12:29	16,200	23⅞	+1⅞	REOP

Three trades at 11:20 caused the stock to go up ⅞ point from 21½ to 22¼. In addition, the reopening trade was also flagged.

The analyst's first step was to check out the news from the previous day. He found that another company announced at 12:15 p.m. that they were going to make a tender offer to acquire this stock in exchange for about $25 worth of their securities. Because a deal of this sort sometimes fails to materialize, the analyst knew it is normal for a stock to trade at a discount until the merger actually is closed. The reopening price of 23⅝ therefore appeared reasonable and it looked as though the specialist acted properly on this trade.

Nevertheless, the analyst was not fully satisfied with the 11:20 trading sequence. The specialist told him he noticed a showing of interest from one broker earlier in the morning. He purchased 1,200 shares at 21⅛ and 21¼. But this seemed perfectly normal.

However, at 11:10 this broker came back to the post followed by two other brokers. They began frantically competing with each other buying everything in sight. Trading was quickly halted. The specialist sensed that something not yet announced was responsible for the activity. He immediately contacted a Floor Official to say that he wanted to halt trading until someone on the staff could contact the company to clarify the situation.

The Floor Official immediately got on the hot line to the staff listing representative assigned to the company. He filled the listing rep in on trading and asked him to find out from the company what was going on. When the rep got through to the company, the president's secretary refused to connect him with the president or the other officers on his contact list. She evasively stated they were all out of the office and she didn't know where or how to reach them. The rep emphasized to her the emergency nature of his call. He asked her to find someone he could speak to because trading was now halted and would not be reopened until the Exchange got through to the president.

At this point the analyst reviewing the trading was satisfied the specialist had acted properly. While he already had decided not to pursue the matter further, he nevertheless was anxious to hear how the story turned out. It is important to point out here that as soon as the specialist determined that something unusual was happening he did not contact the company directly. Neither he nor the company are supposed to discuss directly with each other information that has not yet been released publicly. Instead, he asked the Exchange staff to make the contact. The Exchange listing representative by the nature of his job is often privy to confidential information from both the company and the specialist. He is trained to work with both sides to assist them with mutual disclosure problems while withholding from each side confidential information which would place them in legal jeopardy with governmental regulatory agencies. The listing representative can weigh the value of the information he receives from a company and help them decide what announcements if any, are required.

About five minutes after he contacted the company, the listing rep received a call from the company's counsel who bitterly denounced him for the halt in trading and who threatened to sue the Exchange unless trading was resumed immediately. He mentioned the obligation of the Exchange to maintain a market in its listed stocks at all times and spoke of the embarrassment to the company of the Exchange's decision to halt trading in the stock.

The rep had heard all this many times before. By the intensity of the lawyer's argument he knew instinctively that an important announcement was either pending or should be required of the company. It seems never to fail. Every time counsel rather than the company president answers there seems to be a fire under all the smoke. Furthermore, the louder, more aggressive, more abusive the theatrics, the more certain and the more important the announcement seems likely to be.

The listing rep patiently waited out the counsel. He did not cut in but instead let the counsel talk himself out. When he finally wound down, it was the rep's turn.

"If you are finished with your routine, let's get down to business. I would have cut in on you sooner but it was your nickel and besides you have a pretty good line. It's one of the best I've ever heard but don't bother putting on your show again because it just isn't relative to the problem we are faced with at this time.

"Here is our problem. First of all, it's entirely proper and natural for the Exchange to temporarily halt trading in a stock when an abnormal trading situation develops. A halt in trading is not a reflection, good, bad or indifferent on anyone. The only thing it means is that a lot of orders have come down to the Floor at about the same time and trading has to be halted until the specialist has a chance to sort them out. This is purely a mechanical problem caused by a technical inability for a person to handle more than a certain amount of papers at one time. This sort of thing happens from time to time. All that it means is that a lot of people are interested in the same stock at the same time.

"In your case we have something different. Your stock was trading normally when all of a sudden, and for no apparent reason a concentrated buying interest appeared aggressively grabbing all the stock in sight. It's been our experience that when this sort of thing happens, there is often a good reason for the buying. We find that the reason usually revolves around somebody knowing that something is about to cause the price to move up shortly. Often that something is important enough for the company involved to make an announcement. When your company listed, you signed an agreement stating you would disclose fully all material information. We needed this from you because the Amex not only has an obligation to you, of which you so forcefully reminded me just a few minutes ago, but we also have an obligation to your present stockholders, your future stockholders, our specialists and to the general public.

"From where we stand, it looks to us like something is about to happen in your shop that is going to cause your stock to go higher. It looks to us like someone already has this information and is trying to capitalize on it. If that is the case and if it is as bullish for your stock as it seems to be, a lot of your present stockholders who are in the process of selling at current prices are going to be hurt. We don't want that to happen. Therefore, what I want to know once again is this. Is anything going on in your company that should be announced at this time? This would include such things as mergers, acquisitions, major new products, etc."

"There is nothing that I can announce at this time."

"I didn't ask if there was anything you can announce at this time. I want to know if there is something that should be announced. Bear in mind there appears to have been a leak and someone seems to be acting on the leak."

"I'm not at liberty to say."

"Then I'm going to ask you to put out an announcement to the effect that 'The company knows of no present or anticipated future development which would account for any abnormal activity in it's stock at this time.' "

"I'm not sure that I can say that. What if we said that and the company came out with an announcement of some kind next week?"

"If you're getting paid to advise the company, you should be aware of the various S.E.C. rules on that point."

"There is nothing I can say now. We're not ready to say anything at this point. We're working on a deal but its not firm yet and we don't want to make an announcement for another week or so until it will be firm. I guess you'll just have to square away your imbalance as best as you can and reopen the stock."

"Apparently you don't get the picture. You have already lost your flexibility. You have no more choice in the matter. It's too late for you to refuse to say anything because obviously someone already knows the details of the deal. Not only has there been a leak but someone seems to be acting on it before word gets out to anyone else. We cannot permit the market to act in a news vacuum of this sort. If you had been able to keep the deal quiet until you were ready to make your announcement next week there would have been no problem. But since you weren't, we're not going to make it possible for your present stockholders to sell to these insiders until and unless they have the details of this new deal. Then, if they still want to sell, that's their business.

"If the company refuses to make an announcement until next week, we'll just have to suspend trading until next week. We will have to announce ourselves that trading in your stock will be suspended pending a forthcoming announcement from the company. This may well complicate your situation and we would prefer not to be forced into doing it but we have no choice. Let me know within an hour what you want to do. I'll hold off any further action on this end until then. If you need help with the statement, I'll be only too happy to help you. Otherwise, I'm going to have to set the wheels in motion for suspending your stock."

As soon as he hung up with the counsel, the listing rep got hold of the floor official. "Tell the specialist to keep the freeze on the stock. I've just finished talking to the company and we have some problems, I'll get back to you within the hour."

Next he called the stock watch and surveillance sections. "There's a problem with one of Larry's stocks. It might be an insider problem. Trading's been halted. Get the names of the brokers who were in there buying just before the halt and contact them for the names and business affiliations of their customers. It look's like there is a bullish development in the wind and someone on the inside might be buying in anticipation of the news."

About 20 minutes later, counsel for the company called back to say the company was going to issue an announcement momentarily. It was going to say that they had reached a tentative agreement to merge with another company. The deal was going to be for preferred stock worth about $25 per share. The listing rep reviewed the announcement word for word. He satisfied himself that it was complete and responsive to the situation. Counsel said that the announcement would go out momentarily by messenger to the news services.

The rep promised to do whatever he could to expedite placing the announcement on the news wire. To accomplish this, he called the Exchange's press relations section. "There's an announcement coming out momentarily about a merger. The stock is halted now. Get Dow Jones and Reuters on your hot lines. Tell them to keep an eye out for the announcement and to run it as soon as they can so that we can reopen the stock."

Then back to the Floor. "Tell Larry there should be an announcement in about 15 minutes. It should be self-explanatory and there should be no problems. As soon as I see it on the broad tape, I'll call you so that you can point it out. Wait for about 15 minutes for the word to get circulated. Then, if you have no Floor problems, it will be OK to reopen the stock."

This example illustrates how the Amex not only carefully monitors the operations of the specialists but also of its member firms, their brokers, the listed companies and the investors using the facilities of the market place.

The Exchange's interest with its listed companies is twofold. On the one hand, it seeks to make the Exchange and its auction market as responsive to the needs of investors and listed companies as it is possible to be. It works hard at building an aura of confidence in the Amex market so that companies will want to list and investors will want to trade the stocks listed on the Exchange. It closely supervises members and specialists to insure that they provide good close markets with as much depth as possible.

On the other hand the Exchange monitors listed companies to insure that they get out all the significant news to their shareholders promptly. It makes sure that annual and quarterly reports are issued promptly; that they fully disclose all significant corporate events; that they do not try to influence the price of their stocks with misleading announcements; and that they otherwise conduct themselves as responsible public companies. Of course, most companies, like most specialists habitually conduct themselves responsibly. They would not think otherwise. But when on the rare occasion, someone deliberately chooses to act irresponsibly, the exchange has the muscle to take sufficient and appropriate action.

The third and largest group of people continuously monitored by the exchange are the investors who use its facilities and the brokers who enter the orders on their behalf. As we have seen, it is possible to reconstruct any part of the market on any day. When necessary, brokers are required to make available to the Exchange details on every order they accept whether or not it is executed. This includes the name, address, business connections, etc., of every investor.

Computer programs help the exchange's analysts spot any stock whose normal trading pattern suddenly shifts. They have other runs which spot inordinate concentrations of buying and selling in stocks. The exchange prepares schedules for member firms, highlighting those stocks in which the firm is unusually active. Using these, a firm can set up its own review procedures to determine whether or not some of its representatives are improperly recommending stocks.

Stocks which show unusual volatility are spotted and researched by still other analysts. Several member firms are contacted daily for the names of buying and selling investors when the firm's activities in a stock appear either unusual or significantly above normal.

Virtually every stock on the exchange is picked out for review for one reason or another at least a half dozen times each year. However, the overwhelming majority of these reviews discloses no improprieties whatever.

Of the thousands of situations reviewed each year, perhaps only one or two hundred are serious enough to warrant further intensive investigation. Of these, only a few dozen are serious enough, when all the facts are in, to warrant taking any action or imposing internal discipline of any kind. In perspective then, when you consider that from 20,000 to 40,000 transactions occur daily, this is truly a remarkable tribute to the honesty and good intent of most people using the exchange markets.

22

How to Beat the System

AFTER observing a specialist in action, it should be evident to an investor that there is considerably more to the price movement of a stock than meets the eye. The statistics in the financial section of one's favorite newspaper delineate the quantitative parameters of market activity on any particular day but they give no insight into the dynamics which carved out these movements.

Each and every stock market transaction is the resolution of all the forces that interact on a stock up to that particular moment in time. These forces are in a constant state of flux as actual and potential investors make their numerous individual decisions to buy or sell, to withdraw their existing orders or just stand on the side lines. This continuous interaction keeps the price of a stock at the particular level which represents the optimum price as well as the optimum level of activity. At times, these forces will be in a relative state of balance. Then, the resultant price activity will be reasonably stable. When this happens, regardless of the volume of trading, stocks will show little or no net change from one day to the next and the reported spreads between daily high and low prices will be small.

At other times stocks are technically vulnerable to excessive volatil-

164

ity. They can swing wildly both up and down. This volatility factor is something that affects virtually every stock at one time or another; some stocks more than others. It is not always possible to predict which stocks will become volatile or when. Average trading volume is not a good predictor of volatility because sometimes a stock will move widely on low volume while at other times the same stock will move barely, if at all, on several times the same volume.

Previous chapters have discussed what it is that causes volatility. Now we will discuss how to make volatility work for you rather than against you when you enter orders to buy and sell for your own account. You will see how to enter orders in such a way as to minimize the impact of your order on the market in order to receive the most favorable price.

We will not concern ourselves with theories relating to which stocks to buy or sell or the timing of these transactions. Our only concern will be that once having made a decision to buy or sell, we want to get the best available execution.

First of all, keep in mind that there are three basic ways to enter an order. It is possible to enter market orders, limit orders or crosses.

When an investor enters a market order, he demands immediate execution of his order. He tells his broker in effect: "I want to buy (or sell) this stock and I want to do it now. I don't care what I have to pay except that I expect it to be in line with the latest reported trading price." An investor who buys at market should expect to buy his stock at about the latest selling price or a little higher. On the other hand, if he were selling at market, he should expect to get a price slightly lower than the last trading price.

On the other hand, a limit order is specific as to price but not to time. For instance, if a stock sells at 25, an investor entering a limit order might tell his broker in effect: "I want to buy this stock, but I am not willing to pay any price to buy it. Instead I am willing to buy it only if I can get it at 24½. If I can get the stock at that price, well and good. If I cannot, then I do not want to own it. Will you therefore enter an order on my behalf to buy the stock at 24½."

A cross occurs when someone prearranges to have two or more parties buy and sell an equal number of shares. These orders are then brought down to the specialist to be executed. This device is most often used to transfer a large quantity of stock between institutions such as mutual or pension funds who look to move much larger than normal quantities of stock.

Knowing the general difference between these various orders, it is next necessary to realize that generally a transaction cannot occur unless either the buyer or seller are willing to enter their order as a market order. At least one party in each transaction must go into it with the idea that he will accept the best available price at that particular time. The party entering the market order is the one who resolves the situation at that moment and permits the transaction to occur. If this market order is one to buy it will usually cause the stock to rise in price from the last different price while if it is an order to sell, it will usually cause the price to fall.

If at least one party is not willing to trade at market, the standoff will occur because neither party will trade at a price agreeable to the other. For instance, if the most eager buyer is willing to pay only 24⅞ while the most anxious seller will accept no less than 25, all they can do is create the quote 24⅞–25 and wait until someone else enters the market. If that someone is a buyer, he will take the offer causing the stock to trade at 25. On the other hand, if he is a seller, he will hit the bid creating a 24⅞ transaction.

Therefore, every transaction reported on the ticker has transpired because someone, somewhere, whether rationally or not bought or sold stock at the best price he could find at the moment his order reached the market. That price may or may not have any relation to a computed investment value. The only thing the price relates to is the previously reported market transaction and the orders left with the specialist.

With all this as prologue, the only way to invest advantageously is to correctly time your purchases and sales so that your sales will generally be made at prices higher than your purchases. Then within this context, potential profits can be maximized and losses minimized if orders are entered in such a way as to obtain the most favorable executions. The hints in this book will not help the investor with his broad timing but they can save him an eighth point, a quarter or more every time he trades. If he is at all active these savings could amount to thousands or tens of thousands of dollars over an investing career.

This book cannot help with long-term timing because as we have seen, the specialist has no control over major market swings. These major swings are caused by mass shifts in investor psychology. In turn, the mass psychological shifts are caused by such things as changes in corporate fundamentals, political or economic changes. The specialist's only effect on the price structure is to control in a limited way the short-term volatility within the major trends. In this he is either assisted or hampered by the orders entered by investors.

The specialist therefore does not control the broad bull market swing which might take a stock from 20 to 50 then back again to 20. Nor does he or any other one person or small group of people control this movement. It seems to be controlled by something more powerful than any mere mortal. What can be controlled, however, is the point within the cycle where you as an investor choose to come in with your order to buy. Then again, the point where you choose to sell. If you choose to buy at 50, then sell at 20, you cannot rationally blame the specialist or anyone directly connected with an Exchange for lack of perspicacity. That's your problem. You need help in learning how to time purchases and sales near the cyclical turning points. In my previous book, *The Art of Low Risk Investing*, you might find some assistance of this kind.

But regardless of your timing a proper understanding of how the market operates can put the specialist in the role of your partner rather than your antagonist. If your timing is correct and you do decide to buy in the 20's, the way you enter your order will determine how the specialist responds. In turn, how the specialist responds will determine whether your stock will be bought at 20 or perhaps as much as a point or more higher. Likewise when you sell, intelligence in handling your order will often save you enough to cover the cost of your commissions. Here are some observations Larry made to assist investors.

Over-all Market Conditions

First of all he observed that what happens to the general market is important. If the market is going up at the time you enter your order, more individual stocks will be going up than down. If the market is weak, most stocks will be under selling pressure and drifting down. An up market, generally attracts investors first into those stocks which fundamentally are most attractive. Then as these stocks get too far out of line, interest appears to move in wider and wider circles, to the lower quality stocks as investors look for stocks they think are undervalued and lagging behind the market. During up phases investors tend to enter more market orders to buy stocks than to sell. This is what helps drive prices up. People who might be expected to sell have a tendency to hold their stock off the market for a while because prices are going up and they want to "wait and see what might happen" before selling. Therefore, up markets usually make it easy for sellers to sell stock at favorable prices without too much competition.

In down markets the situation is reversed. Volume tends to dry up because it isn't as exciting to lose money as it is to make money. More and more of the people still active in the market, therefore, tend to be sellers. Potential buyers are either frightened away from the market or they tend to sit on the side lines waiting in the event that "maybe tomorrow I can buy the stock even cheaper."

Individual Stock Trend

Within the context of the over-all market, the price action of individual stocks tends to follow the market. Although individual stocks do not precisely mirror the averages by going up and down to the same degree and on the same days as market averages, nevertheless, in a broad sense they do follow the averages. For instance, between November, 1971 and April, 1972 the Dow and most other averages advanced in price. During this period of time the majority of stocks either advanced in price or, if they were in down trends, they paused for a while before resuming their down trends.

Because of this tendency in stocks, as in people, to follow the crowd, the action of those stocks which go counter to the trend is most significant and warrants that special attention be paid to them. If a stock shows an ability to advance in the face of a declining market, this is important. It usually hints that when general market selling pressure is released, the stock is going to move up in price much more strongly than most other stocks. Likewise if it is weak while most stocks are advancing, it is likely to collapse the next time the market turns sour. Otherwise, if a stock is moving in line with the general market, the correct market strategy as it concerns the average will work for the stock.

Floating Supply

Within the framework of any market trend a stock with a large floating supply of outstanding shares is likely to behave differently than a stock with fewer shares outstanding. The reason is that as the number of outstanding shares increases, it is increasingly more likely that more investors will hear of the company and that they will have neutral to diverging opinions about it. Therefore, the more likely it will be that buyers, whenever they appear, will be able to find willing sellers and vice versa. This has several practical effects. First of all, it makes the prevailing trend of a stock more reliable. Next the average volume of trading will probably be higher than will be true of stocks with smaller floats. With a higher volume of trading well-balanced between buyers and sellers, the volatility of prices around the trend will tend to moderate. At the same time it takes a higher volume of trading to move the stock therefore, making it less susceptible to artificial pricing.

On the other hand, as the floating supply of shares diminishes, it becomes more and more probable that whatever people are interested in a stock at any given moment, are all interested in doing the same thing. Often for fairly long periods of time, interest in the stock is likely to be dormant. What little interest there is, is likely to be from impatient investors wanting to get out of positions that are not moving. Then when interest does develop, buying interest is likely to surface at times when no one is willing to sell and vice versa. The reason, of course, lies in the fact that because of the limited float, investor interest is also limited. Thus everyone who follows the stock is likely to want to do the same thing at the same time.

Because of this, it is more difficult to enter market orders in the stock. Volatility is likely to be high in relation to the number of shares traded causing the stock to appear to move inordinately on small volume and investors are likely to be dissatisfied with the executions they receive unless they enter their orders in line with the suggestions contained in this chapter.

The Specialist's Book
The condition of the specialist's book at the time an order is entered is important to the execution the investor is likely to get. If interest in the stock is good as evidenced by the fact that limit orders to buy and sell stock close to the latest market price are on the specialist's book, an investor can be rather careless in the way he enters an order and still get a good execution on his order. If, on the other hand, his book consists of empty "cardboards" with no orders, reasonable executions can only be achieved with the greatest of care.

The Specialist's Position
Contrary to popular belief, it is not necessarily a sign of faith, nor is it indicative of a specialist's willingness to make a good market in a stock for him to carry a big inventory position. The best market executions are likely when the specialist's inventory position is harmonious to the desires of the investor. Thus an investor who wants to buy a 1,000 shares of stock at market is going to do best when the specialist has orders to sell a 1,000 shares at prices close to the market. He will do almost as well if the specialist has no position or a position he is looking to work off. He will do most poorly if the specialist is already

short a lot of stock and resents having to go short another 1,000 shares to accommodate this latest buy order.

Size of Order

The size of an order relative to trading volume also has an important bearing on the execution price. The larger the order, the more difficult it will be to fill except at an ever increasing price concession. If an investor wants to buy or sell 100 shares this normally presents no problem. If the specialist has no offsetting orders he knows it is his obligation to trade with you and he is generally willing to do so very close to the current market price. But if you want to buy or sell a large block, the specialist has to take into consideration first whether or not he is likely to find investors to offset your position in the next few days and second, what price they will be willing to pay to take the position off his hands. The fact of the matter is he might earn a substantial profit or suffer a substantial loss but the price he quotes is what he believes fair, taking into consideration all the factors relevant at that moment.

What is a large block depends on a stock's normal volume of trading. For a stock that fails to trade on many days or which seldom trades more than 1,000 shares per day, a 2,000 or 3,000 share block is a big block. With very active stocks, blocks of 5,000 or 10,000 shares can often be traded almost as routinely as 500 share blocks in less active traders.

Time of Entry

There is a tendency for nonprofessional investors to enter their orders prior to the opening of the market. They call their broker after they get to work but prior to settling down to their day's work. Then they check with their brokers again during an afternoon coffee break.

As a result of this pattern, most orders entered by the general public as opposed to institutions or professionals are executed during the first hour of trading with smaller peaks of public transactions during the noon hour, and then again near the close. The trading activity of professionals sustains the market during the rest of the day. If an investor becomes sophisticated enough to anticipate what nonprofessionals like himself are likely to be doing, he can often receive better executions for himself either by trading against the crowd or by entering his order when the crowd is not active in order not to compete with these other investors to his detriment.

There is a tendency for investors who enter limit orders at the opening to change them to market orders at the close if they do not get executed in the interim. This tendency is a phenomenon which sometimes causes sharp price swings in many stocks at the close. This activity is often attributed to traders "marking up" or "marking down" a stock at the close but in practice, nothing so malevolent occurs.

As a result of this behavior by large groups of investors some students of the market have observed that on "typical" market days, stocks tend to be strong at the opening and weak at the close. They have also observed that whatever trend is in effect at the close will probably spill over into the opening hours on the following day. Therefore, if the market closed strong today, it is reasonable to expect the rally to continue for at least an hour or two tomorrow. On the other hand, if the market was broadly lower at the close, a weak opening is a strong possibility.

These same students have also noted that Mondays as a rule are often the weakest days of the week while Fridays are generally the strongest. Tuesdays have a tendency to close about even while Wednesdays and Thursdays close higher but not as consistently as do Fridays.

To the extent that these observations are valid it might be a good idea for the investor to buy near the close on Mondays and sell on Friday afternoons.

Level of Trading Activity

When entering an order we have seen that the level of activity is another important factor. This level of activity should be judged in two ways. First in and of itself and second in relationship to the total number of shares outstanding.

With any stock, the less active it is, the more difficult it is for the specialist in that stock to maintain a good market. He is reluctant to take on or go short large blocks at prices close to the existing market because with low volume and the trading restrictions placed on him it is often virtually impossible to close out what might appear to be even a moderate inventory position. Then too, as we have already observed, with a lack of volume, a market has more of a tendency to be one-sided with a preponderance of buyers for days and weeks on end followed by a preponderance of sellers for equally long periods. This makes his efforts at stabilizing the market more difficult and exposes him to unusual risks should the established trading patterns in the stock change. As a result, the average variation in price between trades will be greater when it is inactive as compared to when it is active.

At the other extreme, once a stock becomes too active relative to the amount of shares outstanding, it again becomes volatile because of the large amount of speculators trading the stock for the short term from a very limited base of stock.

Strategy for Entering an Order

To enter an order then, an investor should keep in mind the following factors:
1. The size of his order.
2. The recent average trading volume and the float of the stock.
3. Market conditions generally and in the stock specifically.

With most investors who trade 100 or 200 shares at a time the problem is not as critical as with investors who trade in 500–1,000 share units or with those trading in units in excess of 5,000 shares.

Up to about 500 or 1,000 shares, orders to buy or sell at market can be entered with reasonable safety most of the time. However, anybody attempting to purchase or sell 500 or more shares, or certainly over 1,000 should first review the daily level of trading of the stock he has in mind. If a stock is trading less than 2,000 shares per day he may have difficulty in entering a market order for over 500 shares in the stock and having it executed at what he would consider a reasonable level compared to the current market. On a 1,000 share order the cutoff level should probably be about 5,000 shares per day. For a reasonable execution of larger orders at the market, the block should not represent more than about 10 to 15 per cent of the average daily level of trading.

Anyone who wants to enter an order in excess of the above amounts will probably be better off entering it either at a limit price or using special instructions or techniques that anyone dealing in large quantities should be familiar with. For orders below our suggested cutoffs, an investor has the option of entering an order at the market on the specified limit price.

If for any reason time is of the essence in entering the order, market orders can be entered within the limits set forth and such orders should generally be executed at reasonable price levels. Some brokers recommend that orders of any size should be broken down and fed out on the market gradually so as not to disrupt a market. But, long observation has shown that such fragmented orders disrupt the market more and result in a poorer execution to the investor than would occur on a well-directed single execution.

For instance, someone with 1,000 shares of stock trading at 20 might be advised by his broker to feed his stock onto the market in five 200 share lots because of very weak market conditions at the time, on the theory that this will disturb the market less than a single block sale. The investor follows this advice and sells 200 shares at a time. However, there are no orders on the specialist's book and he already has a large inventory position. If the truth were known, he is every bit as demoralized as the investor entering the order. Therefore, instead of not disrupting the market, the investor finds he has disrupted the market more than a single order would have done. He finds he has received executions at 19¾, 19½, 19¼, 19 and 18¾ for example. The specialist backed away from the trades not only because of his own vulnerable inventory position but also because he did not know the total number of shares that would eventually be sold. All he knew was that every time he turned around, the same broker was back to sell another 200 shares.

However, if the order came in as a block the specialist might have been willing to buy the block at the 19¾ bid or he might have been willing to break up the order by offering to buy part of it for 19¾ and the rest for either 19⅝ or 19½. By knowing the total extent of the selling pressure he was faced with at the moment, the specialist could come to an instantaneous judgement as to a clean up price that was fair to him and to the investor. Such executions invariably turn out to be more favorable to the investor than the executions that result from dribbling especially if the investor sets a reasonable limit on the order.

If an investor wants to buy a stock on a day when the market is weak, it is often prudent for him to enter a limit order to buy at or slightly below the market. Limit orders entered in this manner stand an excellent chance of being executed.

If the market is quiet or slightly higher when an investor wants to enter his order, it is usually best to enter a buy order at the level of the last trade, give or take a small fraction. For instance, with a stock selling at 20, an order to buy can reasonably be entered at 19⅞, 20 or 20⅛. These orders, too, will generally be executed.

If the market in a stock is very strong, a decision must first be made as to whether to wait for a reaction to set in or to buy now. If the investor decides to buy now he should do so at the market and not attempt to play games by entering a limit order. During strong up moves stocks seldom react enough to tick off limit orders. There are too many competing investors around waiting to buy at the market. Therefore if the investor decides to wait for a reaction, the big danger is that he will become impatient as the stock trades higher. At some point his emotions will get the best of him and he will enter his order to buy. Likely as not he will buy right at the top.

When attempting to enter sell orders, the same principles apply but in reverse.

23

Summary

WE HAVE attempted in this book to explore facets of the stock market never before explored, by placing you beside Larry Harkins, a hypothetical specialist, who is reputed to arbitrarily set the price you pay for the stocks you buy or sell.

In observing the manner in which he and other professionals arrive at their judgements of a stock's value, it should become increasingly clear that the prime determinate of the price any investor pays is the investor himself. He has complete freedom of entry and exit into and out of the market and it is the manner in which he exercises or abdicates this freedom which determines his success in the market.

Invetors who can program themselves to act in harmony with the market can generally buy their securities well. If they can then program themselves to sell at levels where most other people are emotionally stimulated to buy, they can generally also sell their securities well. The investor who acts on emotion is generally drawn into a situation at the wrong times and ends up paying prices which are at least temporarily unfavorable.

For whatever reason an investor is moved to act, it should now be clear that prices cannot carve out patterns which take them either too high above or too low below realistic investments unless investors by their willingness to either buy or sell permit them to do so.

In the underwriting sector for example, if investor interest is apathetic, an underwriter cannot overcharge because he could not dispose of his underwriting. Therefore, he is forced to price his new issue realistically even though this realistic pricing might prevent some companies from going public at the time. If investor interest is rampantly bullish, he would be doing his client a disservice not to price a new issue high in line with others of the same quality.

In the after market, both the over-the-counter market makers and the exchange specialists are in effect residual pockets of supply and demand for stocks. They cannot set prices within their ability to do so without regard for the larger market trend of the moment. No one yet has had enough money to contain such tides. All that they can do is adjust the pricing pattern within the context of the longer term trends on a trade to trade or perhaps day to day basis. To the extent that their judgement is correct, they can act profitably for their accounts while at the same time minimizing the erratic moves that securities would be subject to because of temporary gaps of interest by buyers or sellers.

We have tried to show you how the price setters think, how they act, how they react, so that you can make their efforts at providing you with good markets for your investments easier and so that you can learn to enter your orders in such a way that you can benefit from the natural forces at work in the market.

Appendix A

TWINKLE, INC.
Complete Round Lot Transaction Journal

Vol.	Price	Specialist Bot	Specialist Sold	Vol.	Price	Specialist Bot	Specialist Sold	Vol.	Price	Specialist Bot	Specialist Sold
Prev. Close	41										
3,400	39⅞	1,000		400	38	400		100	37½		100
300	39⅞			100	38	100		200	37⅝		200
100	39⅝	100		100	37¾	100		800	37¾		500
500	39½	100		200	37⅞			100	37⅞		100
200	39⅜	200		200	38		100	100	37⅝	100	
100	39⅜	100		100	38			100	37⅞		100
300	39⅛	300		100	37¾	100		100	37¾		
200	39⅛	200		300	37⅝	300		200	37¾		
500	39⅛	500		100	37½	100		100	38		
700	39	400		200	37¼	200		100	38		
200	38⅞	200		100	37	100		100	37⅞	100	
500	38⅝			400	36¾	400		100	38⅛		
100	38⅝			100	36⅞		100	100	37⅞		
100	38⅝			100	36¾			400	38		
200	38⅝	200		800	36⅜	800		100	38		
100	38½			200	36⅛	200		1,900	37¾	1,000	
600	38¼	600		100	36⅛	100		300	38		300
100	38½		100	200	36⅜		200	1,000	38		
100	38⅜			100	36⅝		100	100	38⅛		
100	38⅝		100	200	36⅝		200	100	38¼		100
300	38¾		300	100	36⅞		100	800	38½		700
300	38½	300		100	37			100	38½		100
400	38¼	400		300	37		200	200	38¼	200	
200	38			100	37⅛		100	400	38⅛	400	
100	38¼		100	100	36⅞			200	38¼		
300	38⅜		300	200	37¼		200	100	38	100	
100	38¼	100		100	37⅜		100	200	37⅞	200	
100	38½			100	37½		100	100	38⅛		100
500	38¾		500	100	37½			100	38¼		100
400	38¾		400	100	37½			100	38	100	
200	38½	200		100	37½			200	37⅞		
200	38⅜	200		200	37⅝		200	200	38		
500	38½			200	37⅜			100	37⅞		
1,500	38¾		500	100	37½		100	100	38		
100	38½	100		100	37½		100	400	37⅞		
100	38⅜	100		100	37½		100				
100	38⅛	100		1,400	37¼	1,400					

The entries above represent all round lot transactions in an actual stock during a single market day. The stock is referred to in this book as Twinkle, Inc.

The information shown represents the following:

Volume—The actual number of shares reported in each individual transaction.

Price—The mutually agreed to price for each transaction.

Specialist Bot or (Sold)—The number of shares the specialist purchased for his account from the seller or sold for his account to a buyer in his role as the residual buyer or seller.

TWINKLE, INC.
Summary of Specialist's Personal Trading Activities

| Purchases | | | Sales | |
# Shares	$ Value	Price	# Shares	$ Value
300	$ 10,837.50	36⅛		
800	29,100.00	⅜	200	$ 7,275.00
		½	170	6,205.00
		⅝	300	10,987.50
400	14,700.00	¾	175	6,431.25
		⅞	200	7,375.00
110	4,070.00	37	223	8,251.00
		⅛	180	6,682.50
1,605	59,786.25	¼	200	7,450.00
95	3,550.62	⅜	100	3,737.50
100	3,750.00	½	580	21,750.00
450	16,931.25	⅝	505	19,000.62
1,200	45,300.00	¾	500	18,875.00
660	24,997.50	⅞	250	9,468.75
940	35,720.00	38	585	22,230.00
500	19,062.50	⅛	155	5,909.38
1,325	50,681.25	¼	566	21,649.50
585	22,449.38	⅜	335	12,855.62
600	23,100.00	½	1,005	38,692.50
300	11,587.50	⅝	100	3,862.50
		¾	1,881	72,888.75
250	9,718.75	⅞		
400	15,600.00	39		
1,000	39,125.00	⅛		
		¼	55	2,158.75
350	13,781.25	⅜		
100	3,950.00	½	50	1,975.00
100	3,962.50	⅝		
26	1,033.50	¾		
1,000	39,875.00	⅞		
		40	93	3,720.00
116	4,770.50*	⅛		

Purchases		Sales		Description
13,312		8,408		Total shares traded by specialist
4,904				Specialist closing inventory position
	$507,440.25		$319,431.12	Monetary expenditure of specialist
	$188,009.13			Cost to specialist of closing position
	$185,739.00			Value of specialist's inventory based on closing price of $37.875
	$ 2,270.13			Potential trading loss to specialist of day's trading activities

The entries above represent all purchases and sales made by the specialist in an actual stock during a single market day for his personal trading account. This schedule includes not only the transactions required of him as a result of the round lot activity chronicled in Appendix A but the odd lot activity of the day as well.

*Estimated value of specialist's inventory carried over from the previous day.

Appendix C

TYPICAL NEW ISSUE
Summary of First 3 Months—Specialist's Personal Trading Activities

| Purchases | | | Sales | |
# Shares	$ Value	Price	# Shares	$ Value
255	$ 3,902.62	15⅜		
100	1,550.00	½		
180	2,812.50	⅝	300	$ 4,687.50
1,200	18,900.00	¾		
266	4,222.75	⅞	100	1,587.50
495	7,920.00	16	600	9,600.00
1,155	18,624.38	⅛	150	2,418.75
500	8,125.00	¼	900	14,625.00
870	14,246.25	⅜	300	4,912.50
600	9,900.00	½	850	14,025.00
454	7,547.75	⅝	589	9,792.12
200	3,350.00	¾	719	12,043.25
1,260	21,262.50	⅞	100	1,687.50
1,125	19,125.00	17	400	6,800.00
425	7,278.12	⅛	1,480	25,345.00
300	5,175.00	¼	975	16,818.75
680	11,815.00	⅜	656	11,398.00
710	12,425.00	½	325	5,687.50
810	14,276.25	⅝	400	7,050.00
275	4,881.25	¾	308	5,467.00
575	10,278.13	⅞	400	7,150.00
1,300	23,400.00	18	330	5,940.00
630	11,418.75	⅛	335	6,071.88
940	17,155.00	¼	800	14,600.00
1,275	23,428.12	⅜	1,550	28,481.25
665	12,302.50	½	355	6,567.50
1,115	20,766.88	⅝	705	13,130.62
700	13,125.00	¾	1,990	37,312.50
400	7,550.00	⅞	1,520	28,690.00
100	1,900.00	19	600	11,400.00
340	6,502.50	⅛	300	5,737.50
300	5,775.00	¼	525	10,106.25
100	1,937.50	⅜	150	2,906.25
200	3,900.00	½	200	3,900.00
100	1,962.50	⅝		
100	1,975.00	¾		
155	3,100.00	20		
100	2,012.50	⅛		

TYPICAL NEW ISSUE

Purchases # Shares	Purchases $ Value	Price	Sales # Shares	Sales $ Value	
100	2,025.00	¼	40	810.00	
		⅜	25	509.38	
100	2,062.50	⅝	80	1,650.00	
600	12,450.00	¾	145	3,008.75	
198	4,133.25	⅞			
600	12,600.00	21			
		⅛	190	4,013.75	
100	2,125.00	¼			
100	2,150.00	½			
100	2,162.50	⅝	98	2,119.25	
		¾	60	1,305.00	
		⅞	500	10,937.50	
		22	50	1,100.00	
22,853			20,100		Total shares traded by specialist
2,753					Specialist closing inventory position
	$405,537.00			$361,392.75	Monetary expenditure to specialist
	$ 44,144.25				Cost to specialist of closing position
	$ 43,015.62				Value of specialist's inventory based on closing price of $15.625
	$ 1,128.63				Potential trading loss to specialist on his first three months of handling a typical new issue

The entries above represent all purchases and sales made by the specialist in an actual stock during the first three months of listing. This schedule includes not only his round lot but his odd lot activities as well.

Appendix D

TYPICAL NEW ISSUE
FIFO Journal of Specialist's Personal Round Lot Trading Activity During First 3 Months

Specialist Bought	Specialist Sold	Gain or (Loss)	Cumulative Gain(Loss)
21⅝	21⅞	¼	$ 25
21½	21⅞	⅜	62
21¼	21⅞	⅜	100
21	21⅞	⅞	187
21	21⅞	⅞	275
21	19	(2)	75
21	19⅛	(1⅞)	(112)
21	19¼	(1¾)	(287)
21	19⅜	(1⅝)	(450)
20⅞	19½	(1⅜)	(587)
20¾	19	(1¾)	(762)
20¾	18¼	(2½)	(1,012)
20¾	18¼	(2½)	(1,262)
20¾	18⅜	(2⅜)	(1,500)
20¾	18¼	(2½)	(1,750)
20¾	18¼	(2½)	(2,000)
20⅝	18¼	(2⅜)	(2,237)
20¼	18¼	(2)	(2,437)
20⅛	18⅝	(1½)	(2,587)
20	18⅝	(1½)	(2,737)
19¾	18¾	(1)	(2,837)
19⅝	18⅞	(¾)	(2,912)
19½	18¾	(¾)	(2,987)
19½	18⅜	(1⅛)	(3,100)
19⅜	18⅝	(¾)	(3,175)
19¼	18⅞	(⅜)	(3,212)
19	18⅞	(⅛)	(3,225)
18¾	19	¼	(3,200)
18¾	19⅛	⅜	(3,162)
18¾	18¾	–	(3,162)
18¾	18¾	–	(3,162)
19¼	18¾	(½)	(3,212)
18¾	18¾	–	(3,212)
18⅝	18¾	⅛	(3,200)
18⅝	18¾	⅛	(3,187)
18½	18¾	¼	(3,162)
18⅜	18¾	⅜	(3,125)
18¼	18¾	½	(3,075)
18¼	18¾	½	(3,025)
18¼	18¾	½	(2,975)
17⅞	18¾	⅞	(2,887)
17⅞	18¾	⅞	(2,800)
18¼	18¾	½	(2,750)
18⅛	18⅝	½	(2,700)
18⅛	18¾	⅝	(2,637)
18⅛	18¾	⅝	(2,575)
18	18⅝	⅝	(2,512)
18	17⅝	(⅜)	(2,550)
18¼	17⅜	(⅞)	(2,637)
18⅝	17¼	(1⅜)	(2,775)
18⅝	17¼	(1⅜)	(2,912)
18⅜	17¼	(1⅜)	(3,050)
18⅞	17¼	(1⅝)	(3,212)
18¾	17¼	(1½)	(3,362)
18¾	17⅛	(1⅝)	(3,525)
18½	17¼	(1¼)	(3,650)
18⅜	17¼	(1⅛)	(3,762)
18½	17¼	(1¼)	(3,887)
18⅜	17⅜	(1)	(3,987)
18½	17½	(1)	(4,087)
18⅜	17⅝	(¾)	(4,162)
18½	17⅝	(⅞)	(4,250)
18⅜	17⅞	(½)	(4,300)
18⅜	17⅞	(½)	(4,350)
18⅜	17¾	(⅝)	(4,412)
18⅜	17½	(⅞)	(4,500)
18⅜	17⅝	(¾)	(4,575)
18⅜	17⅜	(1)	(4,675)
18	16¾	(1¼)	(4,800)
18	16½	(1½)	(4,950)
18	16½	(1½)	(5,100)
18	16½	(1½)	(5,250)
18	16½	(1½)	(5,400)
18	16⅝	(1⅜)	(5,537)
18	16⅝	(1⅜)	(5,675)
18	16⅝	(1⅜)	(5,812)
18	16⅝	(1⅜)	(5,950)
17⅞	16⅝	(1¼)	(6,075)
17¾	17	(¾)	(6,150)
17½	17	(½)	(6,200)
17½	17¼	(¼)	(6,225)
17⅜	17⅜	–	(6,225)
17⅜	17⅜	–	(6,225)
17¼	17¾	½	(6,175)
17	18¼	1¼	(6,050)
17	18⅜	1⅜	(5,912)
17	18⅜	1⅜	(5,775)
17	18⅜	1⅜	(5,637)
17	18⅜	1⅜	(5,500)
17⅛	18⅜	1¼	(5,375)
16⅞	18⅜	1½	(5,225)
16	18⅜	2⅜	(4,987)
16	18⅜	2⅜	(4,750)
16⅞	18⅜	1½	(4,600)
16¾	18⅜	1⅝	(4,437)
17	18⅞	1⅞	(4,250)
16⅞	18⅞	2	(4,050)
16⅞	18⅞	2	(3,850)
16⅞	18⅞	2	(3,650)
17	19	2	(3.450)
17⅝	19	1⅜	(3,312)
17½	19	1½	(3,162)
17½	19¼	1¾	(2,987)
17½	19⅛	1⅝	(2,825)
17½	19¼	1¾	(2,650)
17⅜	19¼	1⅞	(2,462)
17⅜	19¼	1⅞	(2,275)
17¼	19½	2¼	(2,050)

Specialist Bought	Specialist Sold	Gain or (Loss)	Cumulative Gain (Loss)
17⅛	18⅞	1¾	(1,875)
17⅛	18⅞	1¾	(1,700)
17	18⅞	1⅞	(1,512)
17	18⅞	1⅞	(1,325)
16⅞	18⅞	2	(1,125)
16¾	18⅞	2⅛	(912)
16½	18⅞	2⅜	(675)
16½	18⅞	2⅜	(437)
16⅜	18⅜	2	(237)
16⅜	18⅜	2	(37)
16¼	18⅜	2⅛	175
16¼	18½	2¼	400
16⅜	18½	2⅛	612
16⅜	18	1⅝	775
16⅜	18	1⅝	937
16⅜	18⅛	1¾	1,112
16⅜	18¼	1⅞	1,300
17⅛	18⅛	1	1,400
19⅛	17¾	(1⅜)	1,262
18⅞	17⅞	(1)	1,162
19¼	16⅛	(3⅛)	850
18⅞	16⅛	(2¾)	575
18⅝	16¼	(2⅜)	337
18⅝	16¼	(2⅜)	100
18⅝	16	(2⅝)	(162)
18⅝	16	(2⅝)	(425)
18⅝	16¼	(2⅜)	(662)
18⅝	16¼	(2⅜)	(900)
18⅝	16¼	(2⅜)	(1,137)
18⅜	16¼	(2⅛)	(1,350)
18⅛	16⅜	(1¾)	(1,525)
18⅛	16½	(1⅝)	(1,687)
18¼	16½	(1¾)	(1,862)
18	16¾	(1¼)	(1,987)
17¾	16¾	(1)	(2,087)
17⅝	16¾	(⅞)	(2,175)
17⅝	16¾	(⅞)	(2,262)
17⅝	16¾	(⅞)	(2,350)
17⅝	17	(⅝)	(2,412)
17⅝	17⅛	(½)	(2,462)
18	17⅛	(⅞)	(2,550)
17⅞	17⅛	(¾)	(2,625)
17⅞	17⅛	(¾)	(2,700)
17⅝	17⅛	(½)	(2,750)
17½	17⅛	(⅜)	(2,787)
17⅝	17	(⅝)	(2,850)
17⅜	17⅛	(¼)	(2,875)
17¼	17⅛	(⅛)	(2,887)
17	17⅛	⅛	(2,875)
16⅞	17⅛	¼	(2,850)
16⅞	17⅛	¼	(2,825)
16⅝	17⅛	½	(2,775)
16⅝	17⅛	½	(2,725)

Specialist Bought	Specialist Sold	Gain or (Loss)	Cumulative Gain (Loss)
16¼	16⅞	⅝	(2,662)
16	16⅜	⅜	(2,625)
16	16⅜	⅜	(2,587)
15¾	16	¼	(2,562)
15¾	15⅞	⅛	(2,550)
16⅞	16	(⅞)	(2,637)
16⅝	16	(⅝)	(2,700)
16⅝	15⅝	(1)	(2,800)
16½	16	(½)	(2,850)
16⅜	16⅛	(¼)	(2,875)
16½	16¼	(¼)	(2,900)
16¼	16¼	–	(2,900)
16⅛	16¼	⅛	(2,887)
16⅛	16½	⅜	(2,850)
16⅛	16½	⅜	(2,812)
16⅛	15⅝	(½)	(2,862)
16⅛	15⅝	(½)	(2,912)
16⅛	–		
16⅛	–		
16⅛	–		
16⅛	–		
15¾	–		
15¾	–		
15¾	–		
15¾	–		
15¾	–		
15¾	–		
15⅝	–		
15¾	–		
15¾	–		
15½	–		
15¾	–		
15¾	–		
16¼	–		
16	–		
16	–		
15⅞	–		
15⅜	–		
15⅜	–		

Summary

Total round lots purchased	20,000 shrs
sold	17,800 shrs
Average cost of remaining inventory	$ 15.82
Closing price at end of study	$ 15.62
Indicated loss on inventory	$ 440
Loss on completed trades	$2,912
# Shares traded at a profit	7,700 shrs
# Shares traded at a loss	9,500 shrs
# Shares traded even	600 shrs

Note: Each entry represents in chronological order the purchase or sale of 100 shares.

Appendix E

KLUNKY INC.
One Month's Summary of Specialist's Personal Round Lot Trading Activity

Purchases # Shares	Purchases $ Value	Price	Sales # Shares	Sales $ Value
	$	30¾	200	$ 6,150.00
400	12,350.00	⅞	100	3,087.50
100	3,100.00	31	200	6,200.00
300	9,337.50	⅛	100	3,112.50
		¼	100	3,125.00
600	18,825.00	⅜		
1,600	50,400.00	½	600	18,900.00
900	28,462.50	⅝	600	18,975.00
1,100	34,925.00	¾	800	25,400.00
1,200	38,250.00	⅞	2,100	66,937.50
1,300	41,600.00	32	1,700	54,400.00
1,200	38,550.00	⅛	1,500	48,187.50
900	29,025.00	¼	2,700	87,075.00
2,800	90,650.00	⅜	1,800	58,275.00
1,100	35,750.00	½	2,400	78,000.00
700	22,837.50	⅝	700	22,837.50
700	22,925.00	¾	2,500	81,875.00
300	9,862.50	⅞	500	16,437.50
4,500	148,500.00	33	400	13,200.00
1,400	46,375.00	⅛	1,000	33,125.00
2,700	89,775.00	¼	2,200	73,150.00
300	10,012.50	⅜	1,900	63,412.50
1,600	53,600.00	½	2,500	83,750.00
1,800	60,525.00	⅝	1,500	50,437.50
1,900	64,125.00	¾	1,900	64,125.00
500	16,937.50	⅞	1,800	60,975.00
600	20,400.00	34	1,600	54,400.00
2,800	95,500.00	⅛	1,000	34,125.00
2,400	82,200.00	¼	1,100	37,675.00
1,800	61,875.00	⅜	1,400	48,125.00
1,600	55,200.00	½	900	31,050.00
2,300	79,637.50	⅝	1,600	55,400.00
2,000	69,500.00	¾	1,400	48,650.00
800	27,900.00	⅞	2,400	83,700.00
2,200	77,000.00	35		
1,600	56,200.00	⅛	100	3,512.50
600	21,150.00	¼	2,100	74,025.00
1,000	35,375.00	⅜	2,000	70,750.00
400	14,200.00	½	100	3,550.00
800	28,500.00	⅝	800	28,500.00
1,000	35,750.00	¾	1,400	50,050.00
400	14,350.00	⅞	900	32,287.50
300	10,800.00	36	700	25,200.00
1,500	54,187.50	⅛	400	14,450.00
100	3,625.00	¼	600	21,750.00
500	18,187.50	⅜	1,900	69,112.50
100	3,650.00	½	500	18,250.00
		⅝	500	18,312.50
54,700	$1,841,887.50			
500	17,510.75			
55,200	$1,859,398.25			
55,200	1,864,025.00			
	$ 4,626.75			

Total round lot shares purchased by specialist

Shares transferred from odd lot position

Total proceeds from sale of stock

Specialist gross round lot trading profit

Appendix F

KLUNKY INC.
One Month Summary of Specialist's Personal Odd Lot Trading Activity

Purchases # Shares	Purchases $ Value	Price	Sales # Shares	Sales $ Value	
75	$ 2,296.87	30⅝	50	$ 1,531.25	
125	3,843.75	¾			
75	2,315.63	⅞			
50	1,556.25	31⅛	20	622.50	
50	1,562.50	¼			
373	11,702.87	⅜			
150	4,725.00	½			
265	8,380.63	⅝	75	2,371.87	
357	11,334.75	¾	49	1,555.75	
139	4,430.62	⅞	165	5,259.38	
120	3,840.00	32	235	7,520.00	
150	4,818.75	⅛	255	8,191.87	
210	6,772.50	¼	20	645.00	
240	7,770.00	⅜	20	647.50	
120	3,900.00	½	82	2,665.00	
215	7,014.38	⅝	71	2,316.38	
50	1,637.50	¾	36	1,179.00	
179	5,884.62	⅞	200	6,575.00	
243	8,019.00	33	100	3,300.00	
152	5,035.00	⅛	100	3,312.50	
40	1,330.00	¼	25	831.25	
175	5,840.63	⅜	155	5,173.12	
160	5,360.00	½	141	4,723.50	
10	336.25	⅝	195	6,556.88	
80	2,700.00	¾			
235	7,960.62	⅞	25	846.87	
307	10,438.00	34	50	1,700.00	
160	5,460.00	⅛	90	3,071.25	
274	9,384.50	¼	181	6,199.25	
207	7,115.63	⅜	300	10,312.50	
560	19,320.00	½	340	11,730.00	
270	9,348.75	⅝	40	1,385.00	
245	8,513.75	¾	160	5,560.00	
171	5,963.62	⅞	110	3,836.25	
310	10,850.00	35	210	7,350.00	
480	16,860.00	⅛	337	11,837.13	
90	3,172.50	¼	25	881.25	
200	7,075.00	⅜	45	1,591.87	
70	2,485.00	½	80	2,840.00	
150	5,343.75	⅝	90	3,206.25	
170	6,077.50	¾	115	4,111.25	
154	5,524.75	⅞	70	2,511.25	
120	4,320.00	36	70	2,520.00	
150	5,418.75	⅛	140	5,057.50	
120	4,350.00	¼	80	2,900.00	
207	7,529.63	⅜	70	2,546.25	
165	6,022.50	½	225	8,212.50	
155	5,676.87	⅝			
		¾	10	367.50	
8,773	$296,618.62		4,857	$165,551.62	Total specialist odd lot activity
			500	17,510.75	Less: Odd lots transferred to round lots
3,416	$113,556.25				Cost of remaining inventory
	$110,166.00				Value of inventory based on closing price of $32.25
	$ 3,390.25				Indicated odd lot trading loss

Appendix G

Analysis of Specialist's Income from Securities Trading in Klunky Inc. Stock for One Month

Odd Lot Transactions	# Shares	$ Value
1. Total shares purchased in odd lots	8,773	$296,618.62
2. Total shares sold in odd lots	4,857	165,551.62
3. Closing odd lot position (shares)	3,916	
4. Cost to specialist on FIFO basis of his closing position		$137,144.00
5. Cost to specialist on FFIO basis of shares sold		159,474.62
6. Trading profit to specialist on his odd lot sales (Item 2 minus item 5)		$ 6,077.00
7. Average trading profit per odd lot share		$ 1.25

Round Lot Transactions		
1. Total shares purchased in round lots	54,700	$1,841,887.50
2. Total shares sold in round lots	55,200	1,864,025.00
3. Specialist's closing short position	(500)	
4. Cost of 500 odd lot shares transferred to cancel out closing short position		17,510.75
5. Trading profit to specialist on round lot sales (Item 2 minus items numbered 1 and 4)		$ 4,626.75
6. Average trading profit per round lot share		$ 8.38 cents

Status of Closing Position		
1. Size of closing position (3916 — 500)	3,416	
2. Cost of closing position ($137,144.00 — $17,510.75)		$119,633.25
3. Per share cost of closing position		$ 35.02
4. Closing price of Klunky stock		$ 32.25
5. Indicated per share loss		$ 2.77
6. Indicated total loss		$ 9,467.25

Appendix H

Interpreting the Information Found on an
Amex Daily Journal Report

For those interested in following the transactions on the Daily Journal Report illustrated on page 000 of the text, and understanding the information, the description which follows should prove invaluable.

1. The name of the report is the Daily Journal Report.
2. The date (04/05/73) refers to the date the transactions reported actually occurred.
3. The Page shows that this Report was page 55 of the computerized run prepared for April 5, 1973.
4. The name of each stock (Argyle Corporation) and its ticker symbol (ARG) are shown.
5. The specialist unit assigned to the stock is shown. Usually only the two or three principal partners in the unit are listed to identify the unit because of a lack of space.
6. The number (357) after the specialists' names identifies the "Book Number" of the unit. This indicates in a numerical sequence that the current Harkins-Leifer partnership is the 357th specialist joint venture recorded on the Exchanges' records since the current numerical sequence began.
7. The post number (07) is where the stock is traded.
8. The number (1460) indicates the approximate number of shares in the float.
9. The first four columns relate to the quotations reported by the specialist and transmitted to all brokerage offices in the world that subscribe to an electronic quotation service.
10. The next three columns show the time, number of shares and price of each transaction in Argyle stock transacted on this day.
11. The "variation" column indicates whether the price at which a transaction occurred was up (+) or down (−) from the last previously recorded different price. The number after the sign indi-

cates specifically how much of a change was registered from the immediately preceding price.

12. The final four columns show the participation of the specialist in the specific transactions involved.

Explanation of Argyle Trading Activity on April 5, 1973

1. The stock closed on April 4 at 36.
2. On the morning of April 5, the specialist was short 2,094 shares of Argyle stock in his personal trading account.
3. At 9:55, just prior to the opening, the specialist was quoting the stock 36–36½. This means that the highest price anyone was bidding or wanting to pay for Argyle was 36 while the lowest price anyone was offering to sell the stock for was 36½.
4. At 10:00 someone entered an order to sell 100 shares at 36¼. This changed the quote to 36–36¼. Although the specialist was short 2,094 shares of stock and possibly looking to cover his position, he is not permtted to buy this stock at 36¼ because his purchase would be considered "destabilizing." That is, because the last transaction occurred at 36, the specialist is not permitted to buy stock at a price higher than 36 because to do so he is helping to change the direction of the market and this is contrary to his duties.
5. At 10:00 someone enters an order to buy 20 shares of Argyle at the market. Since this is an odd lot (that is an order of less than 100 shares), the order is entered on the specialist's book and will be executed along with the next round lot trade.
6. At 10:03 an order is entered to buy 200 shares at the market. The specialist offsets 100 shares of this order against the order to sell 100 shares at 36¼ received and sells the second hundred shares from his inventory, thus increasing his short position to 2,194. The specialist is permitted to sell in a situation like this because his selling will modify the trend in existence at the moment. That is the uptrend was already established at 36¼ when he matched the order to buy 100 shares at market and the order to sell 100 shares at 36¼. Now if he had refused to trade, the buyer would have had to pay 36½ for his second hundred shares because that was the next level at which the specialist had public orders to sell stock. His selling, therefore, helped to modify what would other-

wise have been a ½ point move and helped restrict the volatility to just ¼ point.

7. The specialist sold the 20 shares requested by the odd lot buyer at 36⅜ (36¼ plus ⅛ point breakage on all odd lot sell orders).

8. Immediately after this trade the specialist changes the quote to 36–36½ because he has no more stock offered at 36¼.

9. At 10:17 an order is received to sell 100 shares at 36¼ and 75 shares on the trade. Because an offer to sell at 36¼ is more favorable than one to sell at 36½, the quote is changed to 36–36¼.

10. At 10:25 an order comes in to buy 100 at market. This is matched with the order to sell at 36¼. Because an order to sell 75 shares was tagged to this order, the specialist is required to buy the odd lot, and he does so at 36⅛ (36¼ minus a ⅛ point breakage on the buy side).

11. The quotation immediately reverts back again to 36–36½.

12. At 11:20 an order comes in to sell 100 shares at 36⅜. This changes the quote to 36–36⅜.

13. At 11:52 an order is received to buy 100 shares at 36¼. The specialist decides to sell 100 shares to this buyer. He is permitted to do so because the stock at 36¼ is selling up from its last different price level (i.e., 36). Under these circumstances the specialist has the option to either sell the 100 shares to the buyer or to change his quote to 36¼–36⅜. Since he would like to accommodate as many people as possible, as often as possible, he chooses to sell the 100 shares from his inventory rather than cause the buyer the inconvenience of waiting for a seller to appear.

14. At 12:15 an order is entered to sell 100 shares at 36¼. This makes the quote 36–36¼.

15. At 12:23 the specialist gets an order to buy 100 shares at market. He offsets this against his order to sell 100 at 36¼. After this the quotation reverts to 36–36⅜.

16. At 1:48, the order to sell at 36⅜ is cancelled and replaced with an order to sell at 36¼. This makes the quote 36–36¼.

17. At 1:51, the order to sell at 36¼ is cancelled. This reverts the quote to 36–36½.

18. At 2:50 an order to sell 1,000 at 36¼ is entered making the quote 36–36¼.

19. At 3:00, an order to buy 600 shares at market comes in. This is offset against the offer at 36¼. After this since the specialist still has 400 shares to sell at 36¼, the quotation remains 36–36¼.

Summary Data

1. Trades are first summarized to show that on this day 1,100 shares of Argyle traded in 5 trades which averaged out to 220 shares per trade.

2. This information is then broken down to show the number of transactions and shares traded at each fractional price change. One hundred per cent of all transactions occurred on this day at ¼ point variation or less.

3. The total variation of all 5 trades was 25 cents averaging out to 5 cents per trade.

4. One hundred per cent of all quotations were at spreads of ½ point or less.

5. The total variation of all quotations was $4.00 averaging out to 36.4 cents per quotation. Because of the tendency of quotations to often "straddle" the last trading price, the average spread of quotations is invariably at least twice the average variation.